FIGHT
TO THE DEATH

VIV GRAHAM AND LEE DUFFY –
TOO HARD TO LIVE, TOO YOUNG TO DIE

FIGHT
TO THE DEATH

A TRUE STORY

THE BLOODY STORY OF BRITAIN'S
DEADLIEST RIVALS

STEPHEN
RICHARDS

JOHN BLAKE

Published by John Blake Publishing Ltd,
3 Bramber Court, 2 Bramber Road,
London W14 9PB, England

www.blake.co.uk

First published in paperback in 2006

ISBN 1 84454 245 9

British Library Cataloguing-in-Publication Data:

A catalogue record for this book is available from the British Library.

Design by www,envydesign.co.uk

Printed and bound in Great Britain by William Clowes Ltd, Beccles, Suffolk

3 5 7 9 10 8 6 4

Papers used by John Blake Publishing are natural, recyclable products made
from wood grown in sustainable forests.
The manufacturing processes conform to the environmental regulations of
the country of origin.

Every attempt has been made to contact the relevant copyright-holders,
but some were unobtainable. We would be grateful if the appropriate
people could contact us.

In case we forget:
Kattieleigh Duffy
Dean and Viv Graham Jnr
Callum and Jodie Annie Graham

CONTENTS

FOREWORD
A TALE OF TWO RIVALS

Lee Paul Duffy	Viv Graham
Weight: 245lb	Weight: 252lb
Height: 6ft 4in	Height: 5ft 11in
Age: 26	Age: 34
Job: Taxing drug dealers	Job: Protection
Background: Violence	Background: Boxing
Attempts on his life: Numerous	Attempts on his life: Two
Death: Stabbed to death in a fight	Death: Shot dead by gangland assassins

Two men whose names stood for violence – Viv Graham and Lee Duffy, aka the Duffer – fiercely resented each other. Sworn enemies, they ran parallel lives as pub and club enforcers, raging their gangland turf wars in a frenzy of brutality and unremitting cruelty. Engaging each other in a vicious gangland winner-takes-all fight was the ultimate challenge. Their clash ended in bloodshed, but in the end each man would meet an untimely and violent death at the hands of others.

1
INTRODUCING LEE DUFFY

Lawrie and Brenda Duffy welcomed their newborn son, Lee Paul, later to be known as 'the Duffer', into the world on 11 June 1965. The boy was raised on a council estate in Middlesbrough's South Bank. After his first school, Beech Grove Primary, he attended Stapylton School in nearby Eston.

As early as the age of six, Duffy was repeatedly assaulted by much older boys – if you can call lads of up to 19 'boys'.

And in 1979 a gang of older teenagers brutally attacked 14-year-old Duffy and knocked him unconscious. He was awarded £80 in compensation, but the taste of blood set him on the road to developing his skills as a boxer. Initially these were for self-defence but later, when he became a man mountain of six foot four and 16 stone, he dished out vengeance beatings to those involved in that assault.

West Indian Shandy Boyce is credited with teaching Duffy

how to box, although many say that he never really took to boxing. But later Duffy would train at the gym and spar with any boxer. Every two or three weeks he would turn up on 'senior nights' and knock someone out.

Duffy often recalled the bullying he suffered as a child and during his formative years this clearly played a part in traumatising him so that he wanted to fight. Psychologists say that the bullied becomes the bully.

By his teens Duffy was indoctrinated in the rough-and-tumble outlook that estates like his breed into youngsters and in December 1980, not yet 16, he received convictions for burglary and car theft and was sent to a detention centre for three months.

Duffy left Stapylton School in 1981 with a CSE Grade Three in woodwork.

The following year violence landed him in a detention centre for six months. Then, in April 1983, he was given a youth custody order lasting two and a half years for attacking and robbing a nightclub doorman.

Charges of affray and assault against Duffy were dropped in 1984 when no one would give evidence at court. (Four similar charges were dropped on separate occasions for the same reason.) That year Duffy met a single mother of one, Carol 'Bonnie' Holmstrom, a South Bank girl three years older than him, and they began a turbulent five-year relationship.

Duffy was jailed in March 1988 for four years after pleading guilty to a vicious assault on a man in the Speakeasy nightclub (later the Havana) in Middlesbrough. The attack deprived his victim, Martin Clark, of an eye. While serving his sentence Duffy was moved to 18 different prisons. When strip-searched during these moves he became very aggressive. At each jail he wanted to take over and be 'top man'.

In August 1988, while Duffy was behind bars, Bonnie gave birth to their second daughter, Michelle, and soon afterwards she told him that it was all over between them.

However, on being released from prison in May 1990, Duffy visited Bonnie in hospital, where she was being treated for stress. He broke down in tears and then went on holiday. On his return he broke the news to Bonnie that Lisa Stockell was pregnant with his child.

Duffy's childhood hero was another of Teesside's hard men, Kevin 'Ducko' Duckling. He idolised the man and wanted to be like him when he got older. Duffy modelled himself on Ducko and similar hard men and maybe this is what helped mould him into the man he eventually became, although, as a family man, he was undoubtedly compassionate and cared about the two daughters he had with Bonnie and his daughter born to Lisa, Kattieleigh.

In June 1988 Ducko was charged with manslaughter and given a four-year prison sentence. He had shoved a partially disabled man from Sheffield, causing him to hit his head on the ground and die. The death of 21-year-old Paul Dallaway occurred at a 'blues party'. These unlicensed gatherings, often organised and frequented by black people, sold alcohol and usually took place in terraced houses or disused commercial premises that had been converted in a rough-and-ready way. Once the pubs and clubs closed, people wanted the fun to go on and that is how blues parties developed. At one time, some cans of booze and a few grams of white powder or cannabis would get things going, but then the parties became commercialised and people started to make money out of running events where hundreds of paying guests would pack in.

Curry and rice would be served and drugs would be on sale to keep the party in full swing, while reggae tunes would blast out at full power. Usually an open fire was kept going to quickly burn drugs if the police raided. There would be plenty of prostitutes and illegal gambling on offer in the quieter rooms either upstairs or at the back of the house.

Blues parties were very dangerous places where you could get stabbed or shot, but Duffy chose them as his hunting ground for rich pickings from drug dealers. Soon his reputation went before him and he was a force second to none in the Middlesbrough area. Just the mention of his name would make drug dealers run a mile.

A look at Duffy's past will show that he was much more orientated towards violence than his Newcastle counterpart Viv Graham ever was, and because of this he would receive a series of threats to his life.

Back in the 1980s, when Duffy was in his early twenties, he thought he could use his boxing prowess to carve out a reasonable living from crime. For people who make a decision like this, crime becomes a normal, accepted way of life. Court appearances were an occupational hazard for Duffy and, by 1988, when he was sentenced to four years for affray by Teesside Crown Court, he had seen the inside of a court over a dozen times, and more than once in connection with charges of violent crime.

No sooner was Duffy released from prison than he was in trouble again. This time, though, it was different. He was usually the one to dish out the punishment, but now he was on the other end of violence.

The early hours of a December morning in 1990 saw the industrial district of Middlesbrough disturbed by the noise of a shotgun. In the typical underworld way, Duffy had been shot in the knee. A man was later charged with the shooting and, because the damage was not as serious as it might have been, Duffy started to believe he was invincible. Over time he was called many names because of his violent behaviour, 'thug' being one of the milder ones.

At the time of this assault on him, Duffy shared a home with his girlfriend, Lisa Stockell, in Eston. Gangsters of the old school tended to consider the home as a place of refuge, out of bounds for causing trouble, because innocent people could be hurt. The unwritten code of conduct that included this rule may have applied years ago, but it was certainly not observed by the two black men who came looking for Duffy.

The two men who broke into the home of Lisa Stockell on 31 January 1991 – she was nine months pregnant at the time – were clearly expecting to find Duffy at home, as they had come tooled up. As usual when cowards are given the job of real men, they had with them some equalisers in the form of a shotgun and a 'leg breaker', an iron bar.

Not finding Duffy, these two hairy gorillas vented their frustration on the four people in the house, three women and one man. The intruders ripped gold rings from Lisa's fingers and threatened all sorts of things in their determination to know where her boyfriend was. Feeling full of themselves, they finally left in search of their intended victim.

In the early hours of the morning, a time that he loved,

FIGHT TO THE DEATH

Duffy was attending a blues party in a former wedding boutique in Harrington Road, Middlesbrough, unaware that his girlfriend, her sister, her mother and another man had been the victims of two thugs earlier that night. When he heard what had happened, he was determined to seek out those responsible and got hold of photographs of the pair involved in the raid; rumours have it that a police source passed them on to him.

Soon afterwards the two men who were on Duffy's trail turned up at the party and got into a fight with him. One of them pulled out a shotgun and leaned over the bar pointing it at Duffy, who snatched the weapon, making it go off and blast his foot into a gory mess. He had to have skin grafts taken from his thigh to close up the hole in his foot. As a party piece, Duffy would show the sole of his foot, which still had pellets visibly embedded in it.

In a similarly macabre stunt, when the gunman was on remand in prison, he came out of his cell during association, took a draw on a cigarette, blew the smoke into a trainer he had just taken off and asked people what it was. No one knew until he said, 'Duffy's foot, after it was shot!'

Duffy must have been getting used to being shot at. Just over a month before that incident he had been confronted by a gunman who made the first attempt to murder him. That night, 27 December 1990, Duffy was called out from a club in Middlesbrough's Princes Road, only to be forced to dive over a car for cover when he realised he was in danger. He escaped death but was blasted in the knee with a shotgun. After spending four days in hospital he signed himself out.

From this first attack onwards it was clear that there was a

6

violent campaign to take Duffy off the scene in Middlesbrough by killing him. Because of his stand against drugs on his territory, dealers were losing a lot of money. His situation mirrored Viv Graham's in Newcastle, where his life too was under threat because he was stopping a lot of dealing going on.

In Duffy's case, no fewer than ten men faced charges of attempting to murder him relating to three different incidents. All were acquitted, however, as we will see later on.

Nevertheless, the scale and persistence of the onslaught on Duffy indicates the chilling resolve of the drug barons to get him off what they saw as their domain.

It was in April 1991 that three men from Blyth, about ten miles north of Newcastle, were charged with the attempted murder of Duffy in relation to the shooting in January of that year. Raymond Palmer, Robert Charlton and Anthony Cole were from this Northumbrian town well known for the drug dealing among its small population and for the high number of deaths from illegal drugs. Charges against Palmer and Charlton were later dropped. Cole was acquitted in October 1992 of the attempted murder of Duffy in a trial that heard that there was no real chance of securing a conviction.

Birmingham has a connection with this story through the involvement of Marnon Clive Thomas and Leroy Vincent Fischer, both from that city, who were charged with robbing Duffy's girlfriend of a large quantity of jewellery shortly before Duffy was shot in the foot. A third man from Birmingham, John Leroy Thomas, was charged, along with Marnon Thomas and Leroy Fischer, with conspiring to murder Duffy on that same occasion. All three were charged within a few weeks of the shooting.

John Leroy Thomas was given bail. The net was widening and four more people, all from Teesside, were pulled in and charged with conspiracy to murder: Shaun Thomas Harrison, Paul James Bryan, Kevin James 'Beefy' O'Keefe and Peter Corner.

Then, in April 1991, it was nearly a case of third time unlucky for Duffy when another attempt was made on his life. If shooting could not put paid to him, surely petrol would! In this incident, which had all the horror of a video nasty, Duffy was doused in petrol by a man who chased him with a lighter, according to underworld sources.

The Commercial pub, in South Bank, was the scene of this attack, in which Duffy reacted violently, breaking a man's jaw. For this retaliation Duffy was charged with GBH (grievous bodily harm).

Only a week before the assault in the Commercial, in connection with another charge against Duffy, a judge in chambers had freed him on bail with conditions that barred him from entering any licensed premises in Middlesbrough. On this occasion Duffy had been remanded for GBH with intent on a man called Peter Wilson. It was alleged that he had offered Wilson £2,500 to drop the charges and he was consequently charged with attempting to pervert the course of justice. (A further charge of ABH, actual bodily harm, was brought against Duffy for an attack on Islam Guul, whom he had threatened to kill.)

There was a history of acquittals in cases involving attacks on Duffy. First, Patrick Tapping, who had been charged with attempting to murder him, was acquitted at his trial in May 1992.

All seven men charged with conspiracy to murder after the

shooting of Duffy in January 1991 were eventually bailed. Conditions of bail were strict, but they had won their freedom. Subsequently, charges against all seven were revised, with the result that they faced, instead, a lesser charge of conspiracy to commit GBH. At their trial in October 1992 all of them were acquitted.

Meanwhile, the attacks on Duffy had gone on. In August 1991, on licensed premises in Middlesbrough, he was set upon by a group of men armed with baseball bats. With weapons ranging from iron bars and baseball bats to shotguns and petrol having been used against him, it can safely be assumed that Duffy was aware that people wanted to hurt him at the very least! And, in doing so, they were no less violent than people were claiming he himself was.

A small consolation perhaps, but Viv Graham suffered fewer armed attempts on his life than his Teesside counterpart. But one incident, in 1989, when Viv was working the doors of a Newcastle nightclub, was particularly troubling. Viv refused entry to a man, who decided to get even. To make things worse, at this time the super-tough doorman was becoming complacent with his own security. This allowed a sinister-looking black Nissan saloon to follow him unnoticed and later pull up and wait for him to get out of the car he was in.

The gunman in the Nissan shot at Viv out of a rear window, preferring to stay within the safe confines of this fast car. That is how frightened the hitman and his driver were of Viv. They feared that even the pump-action shotgun the gunman was toting might not be enough to slow their target down, so they were not taking any chances.

Rob Armstrong, who was with Viv, had his city wits about him and he could see what was going on. He shouted at Viv to move. Then he dived on his friend, who had his back to the masked gunman, and pulled him to the ground. For this heroic deed, Armstrong paid a price: he was shot in the back while making towards Viv and shot at again while lying protectively on top of him on the ground. A man emerging from a nightclub suffered slight facial injuries in the incident.

It was all over as fast as it had started, and the black Nissan sped off with its occupants tucked safely inside like sardines in a can. There was no chance these little fish were going to fall out of their protective tin into Viv's hands. In time-honoured gangland fashion, the car was dumped and burned, with its number plates removed, a mile away from the shooting.

Viv survived this murder attempt bungled by a couple of losers, but it was a foretaste of what was still to come on New Year's Eve 1993.

The problem was, Viv was not as aware of his surroundings as he needed to be. He took too much for granted, a habit which in part stemmed from his having grown up in the countryside, where things could be trusted to always go the same way, day in and day out. Compare the scenario of that shooting with how Duffy habitually reacted when facing such an attack. In this respect Duffy was streets ahead of his Tyneside rival.

To underline the point, when a huge man like Rob Armstrong moved fast to protect his friend, he was trading on the heightened instinct for survival that many if not most city dwellers come to possess. Such rapid reactions are honed by mundane, everyday actions like jumping out of the way of a speeding car or darting across a busy city road. They are a conditioned reflex.

It was clear, however, that anyone who was intending to kill Viv could not count entirely on his relatively slow responses to guarantee their own safety. Nor could they run the risk that he might be able to hit back at them with his raw physical power even after he had been shot. This is why his would-be killers carried out their attack from the safety of their sporty Nissan. For the same reason, a vehicle of some kind would always play a part in attempts on his life.

This happened during a spate of particularly vicious attacks on locals. One burglary of a 90-year-old man's home involved the victim being tied up and the heating turned off. He was left for a day until he was found nearly dead. He died in hospital a short while after this sadistic attack.

In May 1998 31-year-old Gary Thompson was charged with the murder of the old man who was burgled, Thomas Hall, along with 11 others who faced various related charges.

In a subsequent murder trial Thompson was found guilty and is now serving a life sentence in prison. Charged alongside Thompson were George Luftus, 49; Geoffrey Smith, 39; David Clark, 28; John Douglas Trattels, 39; Christopher Dale, 35; Paul Dees, 28; William Renforth, 27; Allen Sidney, 29; Diane Hemmings, 43; and Lorraine Trattels, 40. The offences included conspiracy to rob and handling stolen goods. William Trory, 59, was charged with attempting to pervert the course of justice and assisting an offender. He had given Thompson shelter during the time the police had been looking for him.

Returning to Duffy, we have seen that there were a string of acquittals of people accused of crimes against him. One instance was the acquittal, in October 1992, of the seven men charged with conspiring to cause him grievous bodily harm. You may recall that the charge against the seven had been reduced from one of conspiracy to murder. Since it shines more light on Lee Duffy and the world that he moved in, let's look more closely at the trial of these men: John Leroy Thomas, 36, Leroy Vincent Fischer, 31, Marnon Clive Thomas, 31, Peter Corner, 23, Shaun Thomas Harrison, 25, Paul James Bryan, 31, and Kevin James O'Keefe, 32.

The main prosecution witness, Ria Maria Nasir from Teesside. Nasir refused to give evidence against the seven accused and was advised that she did not have to answer questions that might incriminate her. The prosecution, led by Andrew Robertson, told the jury that he was 'compelled to offer no evidence' and that 'Miss Nasir is the main prosecution witness, but her attitude shows her evidence isn't going to be forthcoming'.

The people who attempted to kill Duffy are cold, callous people. They kicked in the door of a woman who was nine months pregnant and stuck the twin barrels of a sawn-off shotgun into her mouth in order to find out where Duffy was and then they robbed her and her sister of jewellery. But it was a pregnant woman, not Lee Duffy, the 'Terminator of Teesside'. No one was ever convicted of these crimes.

Nasir gave an interview to the local press some four months later and said that she would persist with her lifestyle in spite of a series of alleged sinister attacks on her home.

They say that hell hath no fury like a woman scorned. Ria

Nasir put a great deal of emphasis on her family having been threatened, yet, when Duffy's family and unborn child were traumatised, the court process could not help. The Crown's case was that a contract was put on Duffy because he was stepping on the toes of other people carrying out illegal acts.

Duffy, with some of his followers, allegedly broke up a blues party and the party organiser was told to give him the proceeds. This was the final straw that resulted in a contract on Duffy. In the event, the Prosecution reviewed the evidence and decided not to proceed. All the Defendant's were found not guilty.

After the trial collapsed, Lisa Stockell asked the then MP for Redcar and Cleveland, the late Mo Mowlam, to intervene and all seemed well until about a week later, when Mowlam told Lisa that she could not get the paperwork released to her.

Criminal injuries payments are meagre, but every little helps. Such payments for the loss of Lee Duffy were not pursued, Lisa was told, because legal aid would not be forthcoming since Lee had a criminal record. After Viv Graham, a top underworld figure who had a criminal record comparable with Duffy's, was gunned down and murdered on Tyneside, criminal injuries payments were made on his behalf to one of Viv's three girlfriends, Anna Connelly. What was the difference?

One of the reasons given as to why the prosecution did not call Lisa was that, immediately after the robbery, she was asked if she would be able to recognise any of the men and she gave an emphatic 'no'.

The other side of Duffy – the aggressor rather than the victim – is illustrated by the case brought against him for his attack on Peter Wilson in April 1991. The Wickers World pub in Middlesbrough was the scene for this violent assault on the doorman. Wilson, a kick boxer well able to look after himself, was hit so hard that his neck was broken. Many believed that Duffy had used a beer can to smash the man with, but a private investigation revealed that it was his unaided fist that had inflicted the damage.

The following is from a letter, dated Sunday, 2 June 1991, that Duffy wrote from HM Prison Durham:

'Now then, I thought I would write and tell you the crack of late. They've let me out of the block and back on the wing, so that's all right. I can get to the gym now and have a crack with the Boro lads. People thought I was on protection, all kinds of stories flying about. Well, I'm here now so anybody's got a chance to see me, I'm ready and willing!! Everyone has been to my cell asking about me.

'A million "alright, Lee mates", half of them were slagging me off when I was down the block!! They make me sick, two-faced cunts ... The idiot with the petrol is in here, I haven't seen him yet, if I chin him, I'll only end up in the block again, it can wait. Beefy, Paul and Nipper got bail. My Judge-in-Chambers was knocked back XXXXX!!! Bastards ... I'm up at court on Wednesday 5th and Thursday 6th June.

'The Wickers World assault is on Wednesday and that [the assault on Islam Guul] is on Thursday. I should get the Guul assault thrown out, which automatically gives me another shot at bail. And reading between the lines I think that Guul will sack it. We'll see eh? I have just received the statements from the petrol assault charge, they aren't too clever either, some woman says I punched the lad "ten" times!! And another one says I went over the top!! What about me soaking in petrol I hear you ask? Fucking right. How can you go over the top when someone's trying to kill you? Let's see what a judge and jury thinks. Not guilty.'

What sparked off the Wickers World incident was that Duffy spilled some lager over a man on the landing below. Doorman Peter Wilson came over and 'started being funny with Lee', who punched him once. A third party was asked to see if Wilson would take a few thousand pounds to drop the charges. Instead he went straight to the police.

(In a similar scenario, Newcastle club doorman Howard Mills was offered money to drop charges against a man who had stabbed him in Bentleys nightclub in 1987. The stabbing occurred after Mills intervened when someone threw an empty beer can at a fellow doorman. Mills turned down an offer of financial compensation from the person who stabbed him, and it has been suggested that this refusal was the reason why he later had his leg blown off in a shotgun attack.)

As a result of Duffy's attack on Wilson, further charges of attempting to pervert the course of justice were fired off at him when he attempted to bribe his victim with £2,500. In all, Duffy had nine court convictions to his credit, varying from burglary and motorbike theft to GBH.

In April 1991 Duffy appeared in court for a bail application in relation to the Wickers World incident. Lisa went to lend him her support, but while she was walking up the stairs of the court building she was confronted by the men charged with conspiring to commit grievous bodily harm to Duffy, who were apparently either attending or leaving court in connection with a pre-trial hearing. They mimicked being shot in the foot and sang a hurtful song to her. Lisa was so distressed that the police let her see Duffy while he was in the holding cells.

And, while the trial of the seven men was waiting to go ahead, some of them were held on remand in the same prison as Duffy was held in for his attack on Peter Wilson. Duffy was put into solitary confinement while his alleged attackers were free to wander about the prison. It was in the interests of safety for all concerned, but for a man already imprisoned, isolation was a further punishment.

No one disputes the fact that Duffy taxed drug dealers and frightened the living daylights out of them, but, if you had the misfortune to have drug dealers living in your street and the police weren't doing anything about it, wouldn't you want an enforcer like him taxing them and keeping an eye on them?

2
INTRODUCING VIV GRAHAM

You don't really know someone until you see him unwind, and here we need an insider's perspective to help us understand a bit more about Viv Graham. Sharon Tate, the sister of Viv's fiancée, Anna Connelly, gives an insight into the man's domestic life. She also lets us into Viv's working life – a brutal world, just like Lee Duffy's. Yet it would be wrong to assume that those closest to Viv, like Sharon, would reveal any skeletons hidden in his cupboard.

'I knew of Viv,' Sharon recalls, 'when he was a doorman at the bottom of Shields Road. There was trouble there at that time and he just seemed to come on the scene from nowhere. At that time he wasn't very well known and the people knew he wasn't from this area. I think because of that he wasn't liked; he was from out the area … Rowlands Gill. People were saying things like, "Who's this?" and, "Who does he think he is coming across here telling us what to do? He's not from this place." So they didn't like him!

'He wasn't from the town, he was from the countryside, he just came in and started telling people they couldn't get in the bar because they were "worky tickets" [troublemakers] and they weren't getting in to cause trouble ... the town changed for the better when he was around.

'I knew him before Anna was seeing him in 1986. We would be having a drink in the bar and things like that, when he would come up and buy us drinks, so I got to know him a little bit. As time got on, Anna started seeing him and that was it.

'When it came to spotting trouble, Viv could definitely see where the trouble was and if he was there that was the end of it. One word from him and that was it!

'He wasn't a townie, but you wouldn't say he was a fish out of water, although I would ... because I knew deep down that he was green as grass through the way he would treat people and the kind of person that he was.

'He was really soft; he really wasn't what they were making him out to be. But he ended up exactly what they made him. But I don't think he was the kind of person that everybody thought he was.

'They built him up, they came and said, "You can do it." He could use his fists and he could do it, but that wasn't what he was there for. He was only there doing a job and just maybe seeing that they would drink up. "Drink your drink up, lads, howway!" There's loads of people who do that sort of job, and then he just seemed to get bigger and bigger and bigger.

'Obviously, if something did start and he had to fettle them, they could see what he was capable of and how quick he moved. He could handle ten people at once if need be, if it come that way. There's not a doorman in the town that could do that. He could do that because he was a boxer and was like a proper fighting man with his hands in that kind of a way.

'Whatever Viv's dad said, he did. If his dad said, "Don't go there, son. They're just enticing you there as their backup" or "They want to use your name", then Viv would take it all in. This would be voiced over many a thing.

'People wanted Viv to go to Spain as their backup in timeshare scams. His father, Jack, would say, "Don't you get involved, son. You keep away from that."

'Viv would go there for his breakfast and he would talk to his father while his mother made the breakfast and they'd ask what had been happening and they'd [Viv and maybe a friend] just have the normal crack. There was never fighting talk; his father would never encourage him by saying, "Go on, you do this."

'He would just say, "Keep away, son, nowt to do with you, they're just using you."

'Viv would listen and say, "Aye, Father, you're right."

'And he would come back and say, "My father's told me to keep away."

'He was quite green, if you would say that was green. I liked what he did because you respected the way he did it. He never, never took liberties with people. I've seen doormen do things and I've looked and thought, Because there's two or three, look how they treat people.

'You never got that from him because he would come and he would say, "Howway, lads, howway!" and do it in a nice way or whatever. Even if he was approaching them, if there was trouble he would say, "Howway, lads, there's no need for this," and do it in a nice way. He wouldn't run in knowing what he could do with them in two seconds. He wouldn't run in and do it; he'd give them the benefit of the doubt. I liked the way he did it. He impressed me because I thought he was a gentleman and in the job he was in he did it in a nice way.

'From when I first met Viv up until his death, I saw changes in him. In the end, he would hardly ever go out. He would watch videos and ring us up and say, "Anna's making something, do you fancy coming across at teatime?"

'They always had their tea on time because Viv trained twice a day. His last training would be around about, maybe, seven, so Anna would have the tea on for him coming back. They would maybe ring here and say, there's chicken or whatever – do you fancy coming across, we've got a good video.

'We would join them for a meal, and then the next minute the video would be on, we'd be in the middle of our tea and then the phone would start.

'Viv would say, "Anna, what am I going to do?"

'He didn't want to pick it up because he didn't want to ruin the night, but he knew in the back of his mind he had to pick the phone up because he had to make sure people were all right wherever they were ringing from.

'He'd say, "Two minutes, two minutes. I'll be back in two minutes!"

'He'd run and jump into the car and he would be quick. Maybe he'd be 10 minutes or maybe 15 minutes and he'd be back and sit down and say, "Right, sorted, let's ..." and then we'd start watching the film again and the phone would ring again and this is how the night constantly went on.

'As for getting videos and sitting in with Anna, that was all he really wanted at that time. I'm talking about two years before his death, but prior to that they had their good nights out. Being out late, maybe clubbing, and that sort of thing, but the last two years he didn't even want to go out. He was happy with his videos.

'I think that Anna did him a lot of good because he must have felt happy. His relationship was steady and he was happy with everything that was there. Probably the pressure was a little bit too much at the time and he was glad to just stay in and not be anywhere where things were happening.

'There was still the likes of Rob Armstrong and all of them still placed in all the clubs wherever Viv would work. Even then, he didn't really work in them, but he knew that if anything was ever said it was always said in his name: "It's Viv Graham you've got to face."

'So, although Viv was sitting in the house, this news always reached him.

'Maybe Viv would get a phone call the next morning saying that two kids were in the previous night acting themselves and stirring up trouble, saying they were going to do this and so on. Viv would know it would be put down to him, type of thing. Even though Viv wasn't personally in attendance he still had his finger on the pulse.

'Viv used to get splitting bad heads; he suffered them on a near-permanent basis in the end. Viv and I used to laugh because we were like two hypochondriacs, both suffering headaches and thinking the worst.

'He used to take me training with him and his headache would come back and we used to say, "Here we go." We did suffer the same things. I had an abscess and had to have it cut out, then he had an abscess and had to have it cut out.

'I used to complain and say, "I'm sure I've got a tumour!"

'Viv would reply, "So have I."

'He was always complaining about bad heads. When you get an abscess you're run down – it's one of the signs of being run down – so it was getting to him, but you would only know it by him saying he had a bad head.

'Near the end, he was getting phone calls saying they were going to take his life, but he just used to laugh because he had heard it that many times before. Maybe the first four or five times he'd maybe have been frightened, but after a while he'd heard all what they were going to do to him.

'Viv didn't care about his money. Whatever money he had he spent! David, my husband, would try to get Viv to do something with it. He'd say, "Howway, Viv, do something with it because at the end of the day you're going to get older and somebody's going to come along and knock you out."

'We used to laugh about it.

'He wasn't cared because he lived for the day and he'd say, "I'm not bothered."

'David would say, "I'm going to get you a lovely diamond ring because you should be wearing a nice ring. You should have a nice watch and a nice house because your job isn't easy, so you should have something that you can say is yours because of what you're doing!"

'David went and got him a nice ring and he loved it. Viv was over the moon. He didn't ever get himself a watch, but at the time Viv had said he wanted somewhere nice for Anna to live because Daisy Hill [in Wallsend] was a bit rough. They loved it there, the people loved them and they loved the people, but David wanted him to do something because he knew Viv was a waster with his money.

'He said to Viv, "You've got to get something under your hat because you're getting on."

'This is when they started looking around at little places. David was behind him, pushing him into things like that. Nobody else really thought about these things, everybody was only seeing the other side of him. Having a drink, having a bet, doing this, just squandering. David wanted him to make something to put behind, but Viv always said, "I'll never see 40, man. Live for the day. I'll never see 40."

'And now, when he hasn't reached 40, you wonder what was going on in his mind. He said to us all the time, "I'll be finished, me. I'll have my leg blown off; something'll happen to me before I'm 40. I'll not see 40."

'So obviously something was ticking around in his head telling him that.

'He used to talk about what he should have and what he'd got and I'd say, "Look at the life you've got to live, what have you got for it?"

'He didn't confide in us about any trouble. You would never hear him. He knew he could handle it, but it was only his bad heads that he would complain about.

'It used to gut me. I felt like seething because people didn't even know him. Rumours about Viv would get out of hand. It would go from one week into the other and the next minute he'd done this and done that, and it used to hurt me because I used to think, if they only knew him, if they knew the type of lad he was, they would think the world of him, they would have loved him. Because he was genuine and he was a gentleman in every way, even in the way he sorted his trouble. I respected him for the job that he was in because it wasn't an easy job. The way he did it, he made it look easy.

'I remember we were in a nightclub, it was pitch black and we were right at the back. Anna and me were there and Viv was leaning on the bar talking to us, then he just shot from out of our sight. Then I just saw him: he had this man held right up in the air by his neck.

'I was saying, "Eeeeh! He's taking liberties, look at the size of that little man." I said to Anna, "What's he doing that to him for? He's never done a thing. I'm going to tell him."

'I went across towards where Viv had this man. I saw this lass screaming; Anna was saying to the lass, "What's happened, what's happened?"

'One minute Viv's leaning on the bar talking to us and then the next minute he's got this lad up by the neck. Anna thought the lass was screaming because Viv had her lad up by the throat. It turned out that the lad had a knife up to the lass's throat. Viv had seen it from where he was in the pitch black!

'That's how unbelievably quick he was. He grabbed the lad and took him to the door, where the doorman was, and he says, "Look at this? He was in here and he's had that knife. He got past you with this."

'He took the knife off the lad and kicked him up the arse, kicked the lad out and said to the doormen, "I'm warning you that you'd better make sure that people are searched properly!"

'Some time before this, when Viv was approaching the end of his three-year sentence for an attack on fellow club doorman Stuart Watson, an incident happened in a nightclub.

A sex pest in the Studio nightclub glassed a young woman after she had slapped him. The young lady died from the result of being glassed in the throat. Viv had this on his mind when he spotted the same potential fatality that could have happened here, the same nightclub where the glassing incident had taken place. Doormen were supposed to be searching people for weapons and had obviously slipped up. Viv was none too pleased with them.

'The lass said to Anna that the lad had a knife held to her throat. The lad was her boyfriend, but she'd chased him off and he wanted her back, so he was threatening her. The lass was in the toilet with Anna and had been telling her that the lad had been threatening her and he would do this, that and the other to her and she didn't think he would be in the nightclub that night, but he was. The lass was very thankful for the way Viv had reacted.

'Viv had an uncanny knack to spot trouble and get people out of tight spots. It was as if Viv could read what people were saying by just looking at them. I used to flinch when I could see that Viv had spotted trouble. But you could look and see nothing happening, and then you would see him stepping back and making his way to wherever. The next minute a fist would be thrown. He knew what was going to happen before it actually happened.'

3
MEMORIES OF THE DUFFER

You can take the boy out of the city but you cannot take the city out of the boy. This old piece of wisdom underlines the difference between Lee Duffy and Viv Graham. Viv was from a little village and, even though he tried to make inroads into the underworld scene on Tyneside, he still had a bit of the country boy in him.

As for Duffy, by contrast, his streetwise instinct helped him to survive whatever situation he found himself in. He was a chameleon, adaptable to whatever life threw at him, even if still a fatally flawed character!

In one of the many stories told about Duffy, a large van pulled up outside the Empire pub in Middlesbrough with about 30 mountain bikes in it and the driver got out and asked him if he or his mate knew where Bobby's Cycles was. Duffy told the driver that they didn't but said, "They'll know in there," and pointed to the pub. When the driver, leaving the engine running, went into the pub, two men hanging about nearby who had nothing to do with Duffy and his mate jumped smartly into the van and drove off at high speed. At that time a good mountain bike would fetch about £500.

That very night, Duffy's friend went to see his mother, who said to him, 'Have you heard about your mate Duffy? A man pulls up from the handicapped kids' place with a load of bikes asking for directions, Lee Duffy knocked him out, broke his cheekbone and took all the bikes off him that were for the kids.' Tales like this helped build the wrong kind of reputation for Duffy, but then powerful characters always attract exaggeration.

But many believe it is no exaggeration to say that Duffy had such a presence that he could go into a nightclub containing a thousand people and within ten minutes there would only be a hundred left in the place. He would not need to hit anyone with his fists: his fearsome aura was enough.

When Duffy was in jail, his girlfriend and his friend visited him, and when they eventually got in to see him he was walking around alone in a big caged yard. Why, you might wonder. The answer: 18 people in that prison wanted to murder him. To the prison authorities it was easier to ensure his safety by locking him up in secure surroundings rather than putting him in with a mob of would-be assassins.

Another story of Duffy's time behind bars also shows his forceful character. As he was brought out of a door from a little tunnel, he had one joint in his mouth and another one tucked behind his ear. Puffing vigorously on the joint, he seemed oblivious to the prison officer on either side of him. The screws escorted him into a little room hastily assembled as a makeshift visiting area.

'Fuck off!' he said to them.

'Lee, on a visit we've got to stand over you,' they explained.

To this he shot back, 'Look, you've got me out of the cell, but you've got to get me back in the cell. Fuck off!'

The two screws walked briskly out of the room, in no mood to argue with this particular prisoner.

Another time, Duffy's friend Neil Booth decided to climb on to the roof of the Havana nightclub. Off his head with drink, he started to throw roofing tiles on to the street below. Duffy, unaware of this, was in a house around the corner and the police went there to ask him to get Booth down off the roof.

'Now then, now then, now then' was Duffy's way of saying, 'I'm here.' Sure, he had no need to make such grand entrances, but that is how Duffy was. When it came to being involved in running things on Teesside, he could not be bothered with menial issues, but making a grand entrance was always important to him.

Duffy was forever being discriminated against, from the age of six right up until the day he died. He knew he was not going to see the other side of 30, so what did he have to lose by being himself? In time the very mention of his name would bring terror to people around Teesside, but only to those with good reason to be scared of him. Everyone who suffered at his hands had some connection to the underworld, either directly or indirectly. The people who tried to kill Duffy on a string of occasions did not know him personally; they were contract killers working for others.

After Duffy was shot the second time and was hospitalised for a few days, he would smoke dope to help him overcome the pain. 'Come here. Do you want a go of this?' he would say to his armed police guard as he held out a joint mockingly.

Yet Duffy was also a sensitive man, and an extract from a letter he wrote to Lisa Stockell reveals this side of him. Here was a man who had had half his foot shot off in an assassination attempt and his skull beaten with a crowbar. And yet all he speaks of in this letter, written on one side of a greetings card, is the pain and suffering his girlfriend must have gone through when she went into hospital to have their daughter Kattieleigh, obviously without his being able to witness the birth. Not once does he fall into self-pity for his own predicament.

The neat handwriting points to someone who is methodical and artistic. Some of the text slopes down from right to left, an indication he was depressed. The neatness of the hand leads me to believe he was a bit of a perfectionist, and it's well known that perfectionists can become frustrated. Maybe this helps explain why Duffy would sometimes fly off the handle. But, despite these outbursts, he was also someone who thought a lot.

It's clear that his chosen lifestyle also brought with it a degree of paranoia, though maybe this was just a state of heightened vigilance. Anyway, one day Duffy was on his way to a blues party and became paranoid, thinking the people that had previously shot him were there. He drove to a house in Stockton, went in and within minutes returned to the car carrying three guns. To one of his associates he said, 'Here, get one of them.'

'Fuck you with your "get one of them",' the man replied. 'I don't mind having a fight with someone, but if I get caught with this and you shoot someone, the frame of mind you're in, I'm getting 15 years here.'

As they were leaving Stockton, their car was nearly hit by a police van that raced through traffic lights.

'He goes through and misses the car, a Sierra, doing about 60mph,' recalls an associate of Duffy's. 'I said to Duffy, "Go for it, go for it, and let's get out of here. He's got to turn around, he's in a transit van, let's offski."

'Duffy says to me, "Let's fucking offski."

'He pulls up, and at that time he's got three loaded guns and ammunition in the car. I'm wiping the guns and the door handles of the car down.

'Duffy jumps out of the car, goes straight over to the bobby's van and says, "What the fucking hell do you think you're doing, you?"

'Martin Shallows [the police driver] says, "All right, Lee, what's the matter?"

'Duffy says, "I'll tell you what the fuck's the matter with me: you've just nearly crashed into me, you daft cunt."

'The reply was: "Lee, howway, just get yourself out of Stockton, mate, no problem, no problem."

'Another time, someone had a load of cannabis resin in the car and the coppers pulled Lee for a routine check because it was Duffy. He went off his head like he was a loony and they brought a squad car out to give the car a full checkover. They never found the cannabis that was hidden underneath the seat. Instead of him keeping his mouth shut he couldn't.

'Duffy and his friends – one of them was Lee Harrison – were in a place on Normanby Road and someone went in to tip Duffy off that there was a large police presence outside. An inspector wearing a flat cap and uniform with all the buttons on walked in and he said, "All right, Lee?"

'Duffy says, "Yeah."

'The inspector says, "We want to have a word with Lee Harrison over fines."

'Duffy says, "Fuck off out of here now, before I give you it!"

'The inspector said, "I can come back …"

'"Come back with who you want," intervened Duffy.

'The man who owned the pub came in and said, "There's fucking loads of them outside."

'Duffy and his friends knew if they went out and drove away that they would get pulled over, so they got a taxi. On their way along Normanby Road, all of a sudden, an unmarked squad car pulls in front of the taxi and stops and, out of the side of the road, armed police ambush them, shouting, "*Get on the floor face down! Get on the floor!*"

'Everyone except Duffy gets down on the floor. He walks around saying, "Fuck getting on the floor, I'm getting on no floor. Fuck you telling me to get on the floor."

'One of the police officers said to the officer in charge that Duffy wouldn't get on the floor and he was told Lee was "all right". This was an indicator of Duffy being considered too lethal to push about.'

Many people have taken what has been said or written about Duffy as gospel. I've spoken to the hardest of hard throughout the UK and, up until now, all of these people, with just one exception, has turned out to be a likeable character. Why should Duffy have been any different?

Usually it is fear of something that brings out the worst in a man. Duffy had a fear of being bullied, so he got in first. If you were not a threat to him, fine. If you were not a lowlife drug dealer, fine. If you were not one of those who had bullied him from the age of six, fine. It seems that the only people who had anything to fear from him were the evil ones. Some say Duffy was evil, but they are all people who never met him.

Tommy Harrison, one of the elder statesmen of the Teesside underworld, has many memories of Duffy. 'Lee once knocked on my door and said, "I've been shot. I want the bullet taken out."

'I said, "That's not a bullet, it's a shotgun wound. It's lead shot. I can't do it. You'll have to go to hospital because it'll get poisoned." It did poison because part of his jeans had gone into his leg along with the lead shot.

'He'd sometimes go missing for days on end up to Newcastle, at a pub called the Bay Horse. I used to have to go up and get him.

'When the petrol was thrown over him, he just whacked the geezer before the geezer had a chance to pull a lighter out. When they had the gun pointed at his belly, he just wrestled it to the floor. He was fearless, he didn't fear anyone. How many people in Middlesbrough walk around with guns and knives? The people trying to kill him were out of the area and were paid to do him in. I couldn't have seen anybody enticing him into a blues party so he could be killed. They'd have had to do him in. They couldn't have just whacked him, because he'd have come back at them.

'When I lived in North Ormesby, he used to go running every day and this day he'd been running and training. He used to run up the hills, pulling a log up with him. He came to my house and said, "Have you got anything to eat?" Eggs, sausage, bacon, liver, tomato, the lot, then he'd be off.

'He gets round the corner and someone wants to have a pop at him. Lee smashed his jaw, clipped his cheekbone with two right-handers. How do you go and train, have a nice meal and go round the corner and see somebody that wants to have a pop at you? I don't know how you can define that.

'When he got into trouble at the Speakeasy, he was in there just having a drink when it was a firm from Leeds causing trouble and he was asked for a hand and they all blamed him. The others never got charged and he did. It wasn't in his nature to be used, but it was in his nature to help you. If you were in a bit of bother he'd help you.

'I had a bit of bother with someone and he said to me, "Where are you going?"

'I said, "I'm going to go and fight somebody."

'"I'm coming too," he replied.

'He was barred from the town while he was on this particular condition of bail. But he'd help you straight away; he wouldn't say, "How much are you paying me?"

'Lee used to love going out with me. He loved it. He didn't swear or anything like that when he was mixing with proper people. Towards the end, he started to mix with the wrong sorts of people.

'He was going to fight Lenny ['The Guv'nor'] McLean until he got shot. I went down to London. I had a few well known faces putting money up for all this. He was fit, he was bouncing, then he got shot in the knee! I think Lee would have had the upper hand with Lenny McLean because Lee was young and, don't forget, he was nearly 18 stone and he could hit hard. I mean, I knew McLean and Frank Warren.

'I was going to have a go with McLean in 1978 in the Empire Rooms, Tottenham Court Road, London. Lenny came in with young Frank Warren when they were associated with backstreet boxing. I've known Frank from being a kid and Ritchie Anderson. I just thought, if I were four years younger I'd have just been on the boil. Lenny wasn't as big as that in the seventies. He was on the gear. He wasn't as big as he was when he died.

'I said to Frank, "If ever you want anything, then there's my phone number," and I said, "You'll never spend that," and I gave it to him on a £10 note.

'He replied, "I'm not as bad as you. There's my phone number," and he gave it to me on a £20 note!

'And Lenny McLean just sat there and we were eyeing each other up, but I don't think McLean would have beaten Lee. I don't think anyone could have beaten him.

'Everybody knew Lee because every nick he went to, he battered the top man. He'd say, "Who's the guv'nor in here?" Wallop, wallop, wallop, and he'd give him it. He just made sure they knew who he was.

'Lee did a bit of boxing, but it's what's in you that counts, but boxing does help you. You have to train; a Rolls-Royce won't run without petrol. He was powerful and he was a big hitter; if he hit you, then something would break. I said to Lee, "When you're fighting, surprise them." He had power and he had speed. It's not how heavy you are, it's the speed.

'You could rib him and have a bit of crack with him; if he knew you, he wasn't a bully. I loaned him and our Lee £5,000 one day and they dodged me with the repayment money. They were upstairs in the Speakeasy and they were saying, "Oh, the old man's here!"

'I said, "Hey, get here, I want you and I want you," pointing at the two Lees. "Where's that money? I want paying, you bastards, and I want the money now."

'They said, "We'll get you it."

'I replied, "Well, I want it and don't dodge me."

'We were all laughing. He could have said to me, "Shut up, you're getting nothing."

'You'd have to get to know him. Outsiders couldn't get close to him, but if he took to you he took to you and you'd get a million per cent back off him. He was no fool, you know; he was very careful whom he befriended.

'If he was going anywhere, he'd make sure it was safe; he'd get dropped off a few streets before or be driven around the place. If he was in a taxi, he'd have somebody sitting in front of him. There was a time the police were looking for him, he was out of the back bathroom window and he was off ... naked – he ripped all his leg open, but he was off like a shot.

'There was a time he got a dodgy passport and flight tickets to go off to Spain to stay out of the road for a bit when he had some trouble. He went to Charrington's [Brian Charrington of Teesside] garage and they blocked the garage off. Lee would take a car off you, "I'll borrow that car off you."

'When mobile phones were first around in the early nineties, they were the size of building bricks. Lee would drive around in a soft-top car and have one held up to his ear and it wasn't even switched on! I gave our Lee a mobile phone. The bill in the first month was £1,100. I said, "Give me it here." They thought it was a trend, the pair of them.

'There were never enough hours in the day for him, cars here and there, going all over. They went to the Hacienda club [in Manchester] and knocked the doors open.

'They were all running around looking for him in Manchester. He was hid in the boot of a car. He goes up to the doormen. *BOOM! BOOM!* He knocked them out. Lee wasn't bothered about doormen; it was like going for the title, you go through the ranks. *BANG! BANG! BANG!* Just knocking them out!

'Lee was a good conversationalist but, if he were going to be involved in a fight, then he wouldn't talk his way out of it, no, no! There's a story about Lee holding a gun to a taxi driver's head in a game of Russian roulette. He never held it up to the man's head; it was a lie, whoever said it. He just shot a hole in the roof of the taxi before he got out and the man said, "What have you done to my taxi?"

'Lee could drive, but he was lethal! Straight through traffic lights! We lost count of the amount of wing mirrors he broke. He once asked, "Can I have a drive of your Rolls-Royce?"

'I said, "No, you cannot! Sit in the back."

'He should have had one of those little DAF cars where you put the stick forward to go forward and back to go back.

'Lee went to Tenerife with our Lee and they also went to Ibiza. Lee Duffy was like a volcano. He needed a rest.

'When Lee was with Lisa, he was a different Lee Duffy altogether, sitting having a beer, watching telly and having a laugh and then he'd say, "Right, I'm off to bed now."

'When Lee was in company, though, he could take four or five on and, when you're young, you're buzzing.

FIGHT TO THE DEATH

'I was in Johannesburg and was having a meet with a princess from Kuala Lumpur and there's a big bodyguard about six foot five, Greco wrestling champ, the lot, and even he asked me if I knew Lee Duffy!'

4
RESPECT

At one time respect played a big part in the underworld. In the days before smack and crack hit the streets there was an unwritten code of conduct. This ethos of respect has almost died out, but it still lingers on among the last members of the old school.

In order to understand Viv Graham's development as a hard man, we need to mention another old-school underworld character, Ernie Bewick from Sunderland, because Ernie was a role model for Viv. Ernie has been called one of the hardest men in the north, but if you were to meet him you would find him one of the most forgiving men you could ever come across.

Ernie Bewick, not a man to underestimate, was fully aware that he could make all the difference between Sunderland being flooded with drugs and staying relatively free of them. So long as he was in charge of the doors of certain pubs and clubs, he would keep drugs out.

Although Ernie and Viv had a lot in common, I would give Ernie the slight edge over Viv in his handling of trouble and his ability to sense danger.

Ernie gives his account of the two fights he had with another northern hard man, Billy Robinson from Gateshead:

'That night I was called to the door [of the Blue Monkey – rumour has it that Ernie started working there because of trouble with a well-known drug dealer selling drugs and because someone had been murdered outside the club]. I was told that Billy Robinson was at the door and he wanted to come in.

'On that particular evening, it was the type where everybody had to pay when they came in, so I went up, and I really didn't know Billy at the time, and I explained that everybody had to pay to get in. His henchman standing beside him said, "Do you know who you're talking to?"

'I said, "I'm sorry, you know, but you've got to pay to get in."

'If anybody had asked me the same thing, I'd have said, "Fair enough." So then I was being called a "little shit" type of thing and there was other abuse like that thrown at me, so I said, "Look, you can't come in."

'Billy said, "Right, you little thing, get round the corner, you little shit."

'I said, "Well, fair enough."

'So then Billy slapped me across the face and I went forward to go into him. He tried to punch me, I ducked over the punch and gave him a right cross and an uppercut and knocked him out.

'Billy's friends were there, his big henchmen suddenly

seemed to deflate, and I said, "Right, get him up and fuck off and don't ever come back here any more!"'

'Months later I heard rumours that I was going to be set up and different things. One day Keith Bell [who changed his name to Keith Collins] came knocking on my door, trying to go on as if he was a friend and he says, "Look, Billy wants to have a go at you and he wants to see you as soon as possible for a one-to-one."

'I said, "Fair enough, I'll come now."

'He replied, "Well, can you not make it later on tonight? You know where I live, you've been to mine before. Can you come through [to Newcastle]?"

'We went through and for a couple of hours they were talking, so I got something to eat at Keith's.

'Later on the fight was arranged at a gym in Jesmond, Newcastle, which was owned by [former Mr Great Britain body-builder] Andy Webb. Andy was a gentleman, Viv was a gentleman, they were all nice and friendly. I went through to the gym by myself.

[Staggering to think that Ernie was fearless in turning up to such a venue on his own, but he did.]

'I never brought anyone with me. I walked into their camp on my own; there were a good few of them there. Viv got on the phone to tell Billy I had arrived. I was kept waiting a further hour and half to two hours before Billy came.

'I remember feeling cold [owing to the lengthy wait] and Andy Webb was very good towards me; he gave me a cup of tea to warm me because by the time Billy had arrived they'd been talking for about 20 minutes around the corner. I more or less explained to Viv that, if I could sort it out over a cup of tea without any trouble, then that's the way I preferred it. [Again, staggering to think that Ernie was as a calm as a cucumber wanting to talk things out over a cup of tea. Obviously the others there might have seen this as a sign of weakness. Ernie is just that sort of person. Not for one minute, though, should he have been underestimated – it was not without good reason that his fists were called the 'peacemakers'.]

'I didn't want any trouble, but at the same time I went through because, if that was the only way to solve it, then fair enough, and Billy obviously wanted the fight on.

'I went through to where they had the fight arranged. It was a small compartment and there was a little bank that went up. I realised then that this was suited more for Billy's needs than mine. With me being a lot lighter, he could get me into the corner or, if I ran up the bank, I would slip or fall over, which I did at one point when I was fighting, but I got out of that anyhow.

'Billy came up to me, and he was a gentleman when he approached me. The first thing he said to me was, "Ernie, I want to shake your hand now, before we have this fight and afterwards I'm going to shake your hand as well." I shook his hand and then we got on with the fight.

'Billy sort of stood in a boxer's stance. I didn't underestimate him because he's got such a powerful punch, and later on, as we became friends, we had a bit of trouble with someone and his powerful punch proved to be awesome!

'My strategy for the fight was to wear him out and then go in for it. That was my strategy before I even went through there. I stood there, I jumped about a bit and I was flicking punches at him, trying to egg him on to come forward at me.

The punches weren't really very hard; to be honest I wasn't even properly warmed up because I'd been standing waiting about all that time in the cold.

'Billy was throwing lefts, coming forward with lefts, straight lefts, and trying to catch me with them, but obviously I was jumping about a little bit, flicking a punch here and there, getting him to move and at one stage Billy got on top of me, but I managed to quickly escape from underneath his arm and I was back up on my feet in no time. At that time I was only 13½ stone, pretty fit and agile, so I could jump about a little bit. [Don't be fooled by Ernie's modesty: he is still very fit and looks like he could walk through a barn full of troublemakers.]

'We stood, we bounced about a little bit again. He was trying to get his punches and I noticed he was open for a left hook. But something inside's telling me to hold that left hook back, so now I'm throwing right hands all the time and now I'm warmed up and they're coming over strong. I even said during the fight, as a bit of hype, "Right, I'm warmed up now. I'm starting the fight off now."

'I don't know how long I was fighting. I cannot say if it was five minutes, but it wasn't half an hour or three-quarters of an hour. When you think, five minutes could be a long time for most fit fellas. Anyhow, I never took any punches – I might have had to a little bit, but nothing really hard – and I came in with a right hand all the time. I've thrown a right hand and caught him with a left hook, so now I'm coming in to finish the job off.

'Billy's moving around, but as he's staggering over I'm thinking, Whoa, I've been caught with an uppercut! But then

I fell over. It was a good punch, one of my hands was on the ground – in fact, it was the left hand – and then Keith Bell came around and he got hold of my hand.

'I was embarrassed because I thought they were stopping the fight because I'd been knocked over. I thought Billy was now going to run in and kick me because he would have been desperate. I was going to roll around and spring back up, that was the theme that went through my mind. I was confident that that was the way it would go.

'I knew I was vulnerable because he could have run at me and kicked me. I got up and that was the point I went berserk. I tore into him, split his lips and that and went mad and shouted, "*Come onnnnnnnnnn!*" I just literally went straight at him, as if to say, I'm not getting beat by anybody! I was really hyped up.

'Then I went forward and Viv grabbed me, shouting, "*Howway, Ernie!*" and things like that. So they stopped the fight. I was confused because I'd realised Billy had knocked me over, but they said, "Howway, you've beaten him fair and square."

'So then Billy went one way and Viv went the other way and I was still confused, so I followed the way Viv went. Remember, walking away from that, I'd been involved in a fight and I'd been hit and for a minute my mind went a bit blank. As I walked through the door, I remember walking into Viv and he was sitting on the seat and he was saying, "Look, I want no trouble! I want no trouble in this gym, mind."

'I said, "Look, I'll stand here with you."

'I folded my arms and stood beside him. Andy Webb was standing there, his head was bowed down. I didn't know why.

I thought it could be because of what Viv had said or he was embarrassed with the way Viv went on, because he seemed to be like an honourable type of person and was nice towards me and made me feel comfortable.

'I can remember I went to the toilet, came back and then shook Viv's hand and everything and we were all right. I recall as I walked towards the door and went out I could feel Viv watching me from behind; without turning my head, I knew this.

'When I got outside the gym, Billy was at the other side of the door, so he must have walked around and out some other way. He came up to me and hugged me and I hugged him back and we shook hands and everything, just like he said before the fight; he kept his word.

'I'd previously boxed Viv Graham and I beat him in the ring. I was too strong for him pound for pound. When I was young I used to idolise Rocky Marciano and when I used to fight in the ring I didn't want to box, I used to think it clever to take punches, so I knew I could take a punch even though I'd boxed only a few times.

'Getting back to the fight with Billy, as I was getting back into the car Keith Bell said, "You know, Viv shouldn't have stuck that sly punch on you."

'"Ah, I see what you mean," I said, realising it wasn't Billy that gave me that walloping uppercut.

'I got out of the car and went back into the gym and Viv was on the phone and I think Keith was in the other room, although I'm guessing about that.

'When Viv finished, he came over and said, "Ernie, look, Billy was like a dad to me; he really brought me up when I was younger."

'I said, "Look, it was only a daft punch, forget about it."

'Viv said, "Is it OK if I come through [to Sunderland]?"

'I said it would be all right, but I'm always like that. Even when I got out of prison [after serving a sentence for manslaughter] I forgave certain people for what they'd done against me.

'After the fight with Billy, I maintained some links with Viv and we had a few discussions on the phone about it because I'd heard rumours going about that I'd been knocked out for ten minutes! I discussed that with Viv and he explained, "Look, I haven't said anything like that, Ernie." He told me that he had lots of respect for me and for how I went through there on my own.

'I built up a friendship with Viv and actually went through to his house and had a cup of tea with him and had a discussion over different things. I remember Gavin Cook was working with Viv through there [Newcastle] and he came through and said, "I've told Viv that you're not bothered about him and I'm keeping out of it, so here's his phone number."

'He must have been match-making and I said, "Look, I'm not going to back down from him, Gavin."

So I pulled Viv up and said, "You're the one going around telling everyone that you knocked me out for ten minutes,"

'He replied, "Ernie, I've never said that. I've got nothing but respect for you and all I want is your respect."

'I replied, "Look, Viv, you've always had my respect. I've heard a lot about you, although the only thing that put me off was when you punched me, but you've always got my respect, but now you're going around saying you knocked me out."

'Anyway, Viv denied saying it to the end. I remember

meeting one of Viv's friends called McNally from around where Viv had once lived in Rowlands Gill and he said, "Honestly, Ernie, Viv Graham had lots of respect for you," and he went on to tell me that Viv was telling everyone I was "a man" and how I'd gone on my own to the fight.

'There was another lad training with me in the gym and he said, "You know something, Ernie, you should never take notice of what some people say. I was training with Viv once and he's got loads of respect for you."

'I ended up getting on well with Viv, but you've always got to remember that there's still a dividing line and you do hear Chinese whispers. I'd heard stories, how true they were I don't know, but he'd come and have a drink with you, he'd take you to the bar when he was ready and as you go in he'll put his arm around you and all of a sudden it's *BANG! BANG!* and he's on you.

'Other stories were that he wouldn't take his coat off and stand in front of the man. It would be something like, "You all right, mate," and then *BANG!*, so I was advised to be wary of that sort of stroke. I always kept that little bit of doubt in my mind and I was very careful of how I went about it if I ever socialised with him because he did want to come through here.

'I'd also heard that Viv liked to have an audience around him when he kicked off with a couple of lads who he might knock out and then the word spreads: "Viv knacked three lads the other night, you should've seen him." I mean, anybody can go and do that, but that's just the image ... but anyway, it mightn't be true because you hear all kinds of stories about me – you'll hear some good and you'll hear some bad.'

Ernie Bewick is the typical understated character from the

underworld. He is not a brash and egotistical man, he does not stick his chest out and spit on the path to give himself a hard-case image. In fact, Ernie is the total opposite of what you would expect such a hard man to be and that is what makes him hard. He does not have to try; there is no need for such dramatics as I have often seen displayed by drug- or drink-fuelled louts. You can keep the lot of them because there is only one Rocky Marciano in Sunderland.

5

THE DUFFER VERSUS
THE TAX MAN

Lee Duffy. In the north of England the mere mention of his name was once a statement in itself. And the connection between Duffy and Viv Graham ran deeper than the disused coalmines of Northumberland and Durham and higher than the famed Transporter Bridge over the River Tees.

Just as Ernie Bewick and Viv had so much in common, so it was with Viv and Duffy, though Viv kept him at arm's length because the Duffer had something quite different about his nature, something that was sinister to Viv and that he was wary of. The Duffer did not want to be upstaged by any man, no matter how big, and they don't get much bigger than Brian Cockerill, the 'Tax Man'. Brian seems as big as a barn door and, when the sun shines, you can imagine him having to stand out of the way, otherwise the whole of Teesside would be plunged into total darkness!

Brian's friendship with Duffy started in the most unexpected way … as enemies. Undoubtedly, meddling with a force like Brian was a foolhardy way to earn a trip to the nearest A & E department. But that is exactly what the Duffer did. He chose to tangle with a force way beyond his imagination. Brian tells of the run-in the Duffer had with him:

'Lee was bullied at school, the same as me; I was bullied until I was about 13 years old, nearly every day. When Lee was 14 years old, John Black trained him and eventually Lee started working on the doors for John. Lee got his "four stretch" behind bars and he was doing everything, so he was a lot more streetwise than me. I didn't start working the doors until I was 20. I trained up until I was 19 years old, but I was quiet. Lee and I knew of each other through John Black.

'I was about 25 years old and Lee, the Duffer, was going by in a car. I'd just come out of a restaurant and, I always remember, I had my finger strapped with a metal splint because it was broken.

'Lee jumps out of the car with his mate,' Duffy says, "What do they call you then?"

'I thought to myself he was going to say something like, "Hi, I'm Lee, John's told me all about you."

'Anyway, I said, "I'm Brian."

'So I'm looking at his mate holding the bottle in his hand and, as I spoke, Lee hit me on the side of the head with his right hand and I see nothing but stars and fall into a squat position, but I grabbed Lee around the legs and he tried to push me away, but he couldn't, he didn't have the strength. I threw him into the wall and I headbutted him a few times and hit him with my forearm.

'I couldn't punch him because of my finger, so I headbutted

him on the floor and he's shouting, "John, John, get him off me! Failey, get him off me."

'The Duffer is beaten because I'm 23 stone and I'm sitting on him and he hasn't got a chance then, so his mate hits me with a bottle. So I grab him and throw him into the car and I walk off.

'My mate's with me and he's a bit scared of them, so we walk down the road and I'm trying to get to this other lad's house because he was a fighter and worked on the doors. So I thought with the two of us we'd stand a better chance.

'I was crossing a roundabout and pulled one of the metal bollards out of the ground and I rammed it at Lee – because they were following us. I pushed it at him and he fell back and John Fail, the other kid with Lee, ran off and I was shouting, "See John Black and we'll fucking fight it out on the field one-to-one, no problem, when my hand's better."

'Lee didn't want to get near me and he was just trying to show off because he knew if I got hold of him he wouldn't be able to get away from me, so he was standing off and not getting any closer. As I was walking towards him, he was backing away from me.

'Afterwards, I went to this Mick Storey's house. Mick came out, but they'd gone, and then I went to Boothy's [Neil Booth's] house and I said, "Is Lee in there?"

'He said, "No, he's not in."

'I replied, "Tell him I'll fight him."

'So, anyway, I trained. I went to Eston with Mat Johnson. Mat put Lee on his arse years ago. I'm looking for Lee and he's with this Craig Howard. We came up near the police station in Eston, near the garage, and they came around in a green Areg Ford Sierra and I jumped out of my car and they tried to drive off, so I dived on the car and the weight of me started bouncing the car up and down and this made Craig stall it. They eventually got the car going again and drove off and just didn't want to know, so I'm buzzing then because I've won the fight without even throwing a punch.

'About a month later Lee phoned me in the pub and said, "Look, can I meet you?"

'I said, "Yeah, we'll get it on, me and you, any time," thinking he wanted to fight me.

'So, the next minute, he asks me to go to his house for the following day. [Lee's girlfriend] Lisa Stockell was there, Boothy and Mark Miller, a kid who knocked about with him. Lee walked in and said, "Look at the size of him. Me trying to fight him. I must have been mad!"

'He shook my hand and he was all right after that. We ran around with each other for about three months taxing all the drug dealers. There were no drug dealers selling drugs then. It all stopped because we just used to take the money off them.'

This is the first indication that Lee Duffy knew he had met his match in someone, and that someone was Brian Cockerill. If he could not beat him, he would work with him, as a collector of 'taxes'. Duffy had a few losses to his name from fights he had had years earlier, but he was still developing his style and had some more developing to do before he would become a formidable fighting machine.

As a fighting team, Duffy and Brian could have conquered the world but for Duffy's carefree ways and his habit of spending money on his friends like there was no tomorrow. The bond this pair had was very different from Viv Graham's friendships. Sure, Viv had the likes of Rob Armstrong and Rob Bell, but their friendship did not have the core strength to run as deep as that of the Duffer and the Tax Man. Viv was a little wet behind the ears in how he apportioned trust. He could fall out with his friends over the quirkiest of things, which may have lost him some of the earlier support he had built up when he was a maverick troubleshooter.

This issue of trust was reflected in the Duffer's streetwise outlook on those he came across: he knew instinctively whom he could and whom he could not trust. Viv, by contrast, relied more on guesswork and got it wrong more often than Duffy.

But both men maintained that life was for living, and in his early twenties Duffy was determined to enjoy it come what may; as far as he was concerned, any planning for the future was out of the window.

When he was friendly with Duffy, Brian Cockerill was also still only in his mid-twenties and he was to have some run-ins with other hard men in the area. Since then he has come a long way, and his own troubled upbringing and turbulent underworld lifestyle are revealed in his autobiography *The Tax Man*.

One of his close associates told me how Brian had two run-ins with the heavyweight boxer David Garside, a British title and world title contender.

Although these encounters are described in detail in Brian's book, I will recount them for those of you not familiar with them. The first clash took place outside a rave club where Stephen and Michael Sayers, from Newcastle, were present. The rave had gone on for three days and everyone was full of Ecstasy.

Garside had made his way to fight Cockerill and it was suggested that someone at the rave was watching Cockerill's movements in order to report them back to Garside. Cockerill left the place at 9am, after a heavy three days of raving madness. After coming out of somewhere that was in total darkness but for the strobe lighting, he must have found the daylight like looking at a million-candle lamp shining into his eyes. But still he was able to stand up to Garside and, it is said, bit off half of both his ears in a fight that lasted some ten minutes. Towards the end of the fight Garside succeeded in getting the better of Cockerill, who came away with a broken rib and a closed eye.

Cockerill versus Garside II took place in a tiny room and this time Cockerill managed to even the score. It was suggested that this is what contributed towards Garside retiring from pro boxing, although it has also been said that he had already retired from the sport.

What follows is based on information gained from three very reliable sources. However, given the amount of violence involved, I have had to tone it down, otherwise I would have to get the local abattoir to clean up the mess. In truth, it did take some cleaning up.

Certain names have been withheld, not though for legal reasons. Should anyone wish to instigate litigation, they would be wasting their time because there are three taped interviews that back up and corroborate what is related here.

It is not for me to act as a policeman or to turn interviews of this kind over to the authorities. That is why people trust me: because they know when I give my word I keep it and I have given my word that I will not use these tapes to incriminate anyone. But, if you want to waste £150,000 or more in a civil lawsuit, be my guest.

What follows is on a par with *The Texas Chainsaw Massacre*.

The elder statesman of the Teesside underworld, Tommy Harrison, was put in a very difficult position when the twin barrels of a 12-bore shotgun were poked into his face. Even so, he pushed the gun away in disgust and gave the person pointing it at him a few words of friendly advice.

Tommy was ordered by the gunman to phone Brian Cockerill and ask him to call around on some pretext. Now Tommy was not in an immediate position to refuse this request, given the closeness of the gun barrels to his anatomy.

Some sources say that Tommy did not suspect such violence would be used on Brian. Like a lamb to the slaughter, Brian turned up at Tommy's home, where a posse of armed men with handguns, a shotgun and all sorts of equipment used in butchering animals lay in wait.

Brian weighed about 18 stone at that time and, although he was still a very powerful man, he could not do anything against such an evil array of weaponry. He had not trained for some time, but in the ensuing fight he put up enough resistance to prevent his life being taken.

The bloodletting lasted for some while, during which time Brian's legs were so badly hacked and his head smashed to such an unsightly mess that Tommy's home was left resembling a house of horrors.

During this sustained butchery a man familiar to Brian – not Lee Duffy – came in and tried, unsuccessfully, to break his jaw in an attack of vengeance. Not a single bone in Brian's body was broken, but his head and legs were a mishmash and he should have been dead. A lesser mortal than Brian may well have been undertaker's wages, but Brian managed to dodge the coffin. Some time later one of the attackers paid compensation to Tommy Harrison to cover the clean-up of his home.

A number of people were arrested and remanded in custody in connection with this totally unforgivable attack. But, although Brian knew his attackers, he would make no statements and so no one was ever charged with this brutal and savage revenge attack carried out by some of the more familiar underworld characters from Tyneside, Sunderland and Teesside.

Some time later, when Brian had recovered from the ordeal, he was given a prison sentence of two and half years for motoring offences and in jail he met up with his main assailant. An apology was made to Brian because, it was said, those responsible were 'misinformed' about the situation.

Brian was familiar with the rave scene in the North-East and his recollections give us insight into what it was like to work the doors at the clubs:

'I remember how I met Sunderland's Ernie Bewick when Gary Robb had all the rave clubs and Ernie was brought down by him because I was in Stockton and Gary wanted to open a rave club there. I said, "You're not opening a rave club down here unless you pay me some money every night to open this club because it's my area, so you're not coming down here."

'The night come for everyone to go to the rave club and I just told everyone not to go, so only about 20 people turned up. So they brought Ernie Bewick down to fight me, so I went down to fight this Ernie Bewick character. I got there and we ended up shaking hands. He was the nicest person I've ever met, sound as a pound, great.

'I used to go and see him every weekend up there in Sunderland. Ernie said, "I haven't come down for trouble, I'm just getting a few hundred quid on the door. It's your door, it's not my door."

'They were devastated because they had to pay Ernie a wage and they had to pay me a wage. They used to pay me £1 for everyone that went in. Because there were only 20 people in they thought nothing of it, but the next Monday there were over 2,000 people in, because I got all the kids to come. I remember it was a Bank Holiday and Ernie used to come down till about six o'clock. We used to mess about on the door with the [boxing] pads and things; he was a nice man, Ernie. The night he killed that lad Tony Waters, he phoned me and I said he should come down.

'Ernie had trouble in Sunderland when Garside was brought in, but they didn't fight. Ernie fronted him and then another time the Sayers came and they tried to beat Ernie, but Ernie had about 200 lads waiting in the car park – he had some pull in Sunderland.

'The Sayers didn't turn up when Garside was there because they were wary of Ernie. I knew Ernie and I knew them, so I was trying to sort it out. I would go around the clubs with Ernie to meet the lads and that. I even met Gina G, the pop singer.

'Paul Ashton from Gateshead came into one of my clubs when I was in jail with his mate Monkey Lyons [Paul Lyons]. Well, it wasn't my club, but I was in charge of security and he comes in and says that Paul's putting a wage away for me for when I got out; he was all right with me like that.

'Paul had a fight with Viv Graham and he was saying, "Fucking make him stand still," because Viv kept jumping around. Viv was only 15 stone at the time, and Paul was over 20 stone. I was inside with Paul and he wasn't strong. I was curling more on the bar than he was benching. Paul could take a good shot on the chin, but he wasn't very clever with his hands.

'I remember when the armed police came for me because I was accused of having a couple of people shot in the town. About 17 cars full of armed police pulled up. I was in my car and I just drove off. They got me for dangerous driving, but I said I was in fear of my life, which I was; they gave me two and a half years. The thing is, they would always come with an armed-response unit for the likes of me. But all they had to do was be polite. Manners cost nothing.

'When I go out I try to be nice to everyone. When Viv and Lee went out, everyone would be frightened of them and they loved that. Lee used to love going into a club and emptying it. What's the point of that?

'Lee used to give people a punch and I said, "What will happen is that, one day, one of those young kids you hit who's 18 or 19 years old now is going to be 30-odd and when you're about 50 he's going to give you a good hiding."

'Obviously he never made that age. The night he died, they were spitting on him and saying things like, "Die, you bastard." As for, Allo [David Allison], I beat him up after it and he never came out for six months after that.

'What happened was, Allo was fighting with a lad in a pub and he was hitting the lad in the face with a stool and I thought he was going to get done for murder if he kept it up, so I broke it up. As I broke it up, he turned on me, so I gave him the biggest hiding he's had in his life. I knocked him out, woke him up and knocked him out again and turned him around and gave him a kick up the arse.

'How it happened was, I'd knocked him out inside the pub and I said, "There's no room in here."

'We went outside, he ran at me and I caught him with two body shots and a left hook to the head and I knocked him out.

'I remember Lee and me went to one dealer's house in Eston and there was about seven locks on the door and Lee said, "Big fella, get this door open." I kicked the door and my leg got stuck in it and he said, "It's on top! It's on top!"

'"My leg's stuck in this door," that was his favourite saying, and he'd wind me up into thinking the police were coming.

'He was a get for borrowing cars off people. He borrowed this car off a lad, a convertible, and he's going down to Middlesbrough, flying down the road, when he only goes and opens the hood! As we were driving, it just blows off and blew away down the street and he just kept on driving.

'Another time we were in this car and it stalled at the lights and he said, "Ah, fuck it" and just left the car at the light. He did it loads of times. He used to take cars off people and just leave them in the middle of the town. It would run out of petrol, he wouldn't put petrol in, he'd just jump on a bus. He was mad.

'What I liked about Lee was that, after we had the fight in Redcar, some months later he came over and he sat and, as he talked, he gesticulated with his hands and he said, "You know that day we had the fight was the first time I knew I was beaten and, for six weeks, I couldn't believe I got beat."

'Lee had only been out of jail for a few weeks and he was with this John Fail character and as they were driving along he said to Lee, "Look at the size of this fucker. Would you have a go at him, Lee?" So it was Lee being wound up by others and it seemed easy for people to do. John Black used to say he was like a clockwork mouse: wind Lee up and he was away.

'So, when Lee and me got to be friends, Lee said to John Fail, "I've made it up with the big fella now, so now it's your problem."

'I walked into Fail's house and said, "And you!" I wasn't going to hit him. I just shouted at him and he went white.

'With Lee, though, he'd be off doing the fighting for others and that was the difference between him and me. People would get him into Newcastle and fill him full of Ecstasy and just have him running about taxing people. He might collect, say, three grand and he'd get one and they'd get the other two and it was him doing the taxing; he was just used really.

'After being in the jail for four years, Lee came out and he was just enjoying himself being in all the clubs, and having everyone talking about him and he loved to have a fight every night so that everyone would talk about it the next day. He loved that.

'We used to go on the [boxing] pads with John Black or John Dryden and, when you're a big lad, you hit the pads hard, so that causes the trainer to pull them back a bit, otherwise it hurts their shoulders over the years. They used to pull the pads back and Lee would say, "Stop doing that," because he used to like people being able to hear the big thud of the punch.

'At times when I've had trouble, though, I've had to handle it differently. Stu Watson came down here with Stevie Abadom, Stevie Hammer [Stevie Eastman] and all them, about 50 of them came down, a big busload of them, and they came into one of the raves where I was and they all stood in the door and I shouted, "What the fuck are you doing in here?"

'Stuey Watson was sitting down, he didn't want to know. I went upstairs and came down, and there must have been about 200 of them; we had all the Sunderland crew come down and the lads in the place and I said, "If you don't go now, you won't be able to walk." They never came back.

'I've had guns pulled on me. You just have to confront people: "Come on then, you wanker." You know they're not going to do it, you just know that when it's certain people it's all bullshit. There was a lad here, Speedy. If he'd pulled a gun out, he'd have shot you. He used to work with me and he got killed, he got shot. I was working it out the other day: there was about ten of us, all top fighters: Viv Graham, Lee Duffy, Speedy and others – they're all dead or in jail.'

Brian is also featured on the underworld 'hire a Crimebiz star' website www.crimebiz.com.

6
WORKING THE DOORS

S ome readers may be unfamiliar with the incident that took place in September 1989 in Hobo's nightclub in Newcastle. In a totally unprovoked attack, Viv Graham attacked doorman Stuart Watson. CCTV video cameras caught the incident, which was also witnessed by two undercover police officers who did nothing to intervene.

Just as the Duffer was used like a clockwork mouse, so it was with Viv. Point and go! These men were easy to manipulate, but whether it was their trusting qualities or their ambition to climb the ladder in their profession that made them so easy to control we will never know.

Stuart Watson has spoken of the brutal attack, the circumstances surrounding the build-up to it and why he could not retaliate. A full account of the incident, in which Watson managed to humiliate Viv by taking some of his best shots without returning any and still not going down, appears in my paperback *Viv Graham*. But, for those of you new to this sort of book, let's take a brief look at it. Stu takes up the story:

'One of the doormen came and told me that Viv and his team were at the door. I exclaimed, "At the door?" So, when I went in, they said that Viv wasn't at the door but actually in the foyer of the club.

'I said, "Who's let the fuckers in?"'

'A voice behind me, Viv's, boomed, "*Watson!*"'

'I turned around and he gave me a left hand straight away. I went backwards and the rest of them, five or six of them, stood around me and were goading Viv: "Go on, Viv, do him! Kill him! Kill him! Do him!"

'I knew two or three of them were blade merchants and I knew they'd be tooled up to the teeth.

'Soon as he hit me, I knew he hadn't done anything with me. I was going to have a shot, but I could see I was in a no-win situation with him, especially when the doormen who were supposed to be standing with me fucked off out of the door. They dropped me like a hot pebble. My girlfriend was there and she could be heard squealing in the background when the court played the video footage at Viv's trial. One of the doormen had hold of her – she wanted to intervene. I'm married to her now.

'Viv is still giving it to me, batting me, and at the finish we burst into the club itself and he still couldn't put me on my arse. Viv, by this time, was running out of puff and he pleads to me, "Go down! Go down, man!"

'The others who were with Viv had kicked open the fire-exit doors by this time and everybody had made a big space for them and they were shouting to him, "Get him outside! We'll kill him!"

'Viv was still shouting at me, "*Go down! Go down!*"

'Viv was more concerned at what was going to happen because he didn't have the arse for it, because, if they had killed me or stuck me, then he was in the shit with them and he knew it. I didn't go down, though. I kept hold of the spiral staircase. He didn't hurt me, but they were like a pack of dogs and jumped in and started punching and kicking me. Viv stopped it; he was shouting, "*He's had enough! He's had enough! That's it!*"

'I was all cut and Viv was looking worried. I said, "Is that it then? Are you finished?"

'My then girlfriend, Sharon, was crying her eyes out. I said, "I'm all right, they haven't hurt me. I'm all right." I went to the toilet to clean my face up and then got in the car and went to hospital to have a few stitches put in. That happened on the Friday or Saturday night and I was back at work on the Monday. Davie Lancaster was also convicted in relation to the assualt; he was the instigator. He's a little man with a big mouth and is known for liking to throw fuel on the fire. I've never professed to be anybody; I'm just a man off the streets.

'I was one who wouldn't bow down to them. If I was given a job to do and they asked me to do a job and I was being paid to do that job, then I did the job and, if they didn't want them in the club, then I'd keep them out.

'After that I was arrested three times for perverting the course of justice because I had a meeting with John Sayers, which the police knew about. And he, Sayers, started out by telling me that I should do this and do that. He didn't ask me at first. I said, "You don't tell me to do nothing. Ask me and then we might get somewhere, but don't tell me." Dodgy Ray Hewitson, a close friend of Viv, was there at the meeting.

'I said to the police that I threw the first punch, but of course it was on video and they weren't having any of it. I made an affidavit saying I'd started the fight. [Stuart Watson refused to allow his medical records to be used in court and did not give evidence at the court hearing when Viv and his associates faced charges for assault. It can also be said that the police brought the action without consulting Watson, which they are allowed to do.]

'When Viv came home on a home leave from his three-year sentence, he had a big party. The whole lot of them were there and I went down and showed my face. Dodgy Ray said, "He's out, do you want to break the ice?"

'I replied, "I'm not bothered about going down."

'They were all in Macey's and I went down. As soon as I walked in the front doors, you could have heard a pin drop. The whole place went dead quiet.

'After that, Viv and me were working together at Rockshots nightclub. Dodgy Ray was the go-between for the two of us. Every time Viv and me were there, you could cut the atmosphere with a knife. I could tell that Viv was dubious of me and he wasn't sure if he could take my shots or not and he was always doubtful.

'So, when we're working Rockshots together, he was getting X amount of pounds and I'm getting X amount of pounds and he was coming in once every two weeks, three weeks, and I was there like a mug standing on the door and he's getting the same money as me! So they say they want the West End lot kept out because they were making a nuisance of themselves and some of them were doing what they wanted.

'They were kept out good style and not one of them got in. Viv was half pally with the West End lot at the time. It was getting to the point that I was fighting nearly every other day on the door and I was getting threats to kill: "You're going to get shot" and all the usual shite.

'Then Viv was away for six weeks and I still had his money and then Dodgy Ray said, "Viv wants his money!"

'I replied, "Tell Viv he's not getting his fucking money!"

'He says, "He's not going to be happy!"

'My reply was: "Tell him I'm not happy, me doing his fucking work and he's getting the same money. Tell him he's not getting it!"

'So he says, "You know what he'll be like!"

'I replied, "I don't give a fuck, he's not getting it. I'm not going to do his job on top of mine. I couldn't give a fuck what he says."

'Dodgy Ray went to see Viv and he half accepted it and told Dodgy Ray, "Tell him he can keep the cunt for his fucking self!"

'So I pulled a few more lads in rather than me keep his money. I felt a little bit more secure and I had some decent lads with me. Viv was up at Madison's, say, three or four times a year or so and he'd phone Rockshots up and he'd say to me, "People's telling me I can't fucking do you!"

'I said, "Who's telling you this?"

'He replied, "People told me that!"

'I asked, "Well, who the fuck is it?"

'He's giving it the big one on the phone, so I said, "Who's saying this?"

'It turned out it was Mackem Tommy, who used to work for me, then he went to work for Viv up at Madison's.

'Viv was still on the phone, saying, "He told me I didn't drop you."

'I said to him, "Well, you didn't fucking drop me!"

'He said, "I'll tell you what, I'm going to come down."

'So I told him to come down, "but there's just going to be trouble, but I'll tell you what I'll do, I'm going to come to your house tomorrow."

'I went to his house with Geoff Brown because Geoff knew where he lived. I went there, knocked on the door, he answered all apologetic and shaking my hand and that.

'I said, "What the fuck's the matter with you? If you're going to listen to people, then we're going to be at each other's throats all the time!" And he said, "Aye, I know, I know."

'Three or four months would pass and then he'd be on the phone again, the same fucking scenario! Obviously it was eating him away that he couldn't put me down.

'We were once in Rockshots when we used to work together and Dodgy Ray comes across and says, "Stu, Viv wants you to go over and knock that kid out."

'I said, "Viv wants me to go and do what?" I wasn't doing Viv's dirty work, so I said, "Tell fucking Viv to do it himself. I'm not his fucking monkey. Tell him to fucking do it!"

'He must have thought I was going to work for him. I didn't work *for* anyone, I worked *with* them.

'I remember when I was at the gym with a friend of mine called Todd, and Viv came in and he said that he wanted to see me outside. So we're standing at the front of the gym and he says to me, "I want £15,000 off you or Adrian."

'He wanted this for his part in keeping trouble out of Rockshots. I said, "You're getting nothing out of me!" This was two years after he had left Rockshots; he was short of money and he was a gambler.

'Todd comes out of the gym and Viv says to him, "What are you fucking coming out for?" Viv went to throw a punch at Todd and I grabbed hold of Viv when he went forward to punch him and pulled him back and he said to me, "Don't you fucking jump on my back!"

'I said, "Jump on your back! I haven't jumped on your fucking back. It's got fuck all to do with him, it's between me and you."

'Viv then said, "Get round the fucking back with me!"

'I told him, "Anything you've got to do with me, you can do round the front. I'm going round no back! I don't know who the fuck's round there."

'Viv repeated, "I want 15 grand off you."

'My reply was: "You're getting fuck all off me. I'll ask Adrian about it and, if Adrian doesn't know anything about it, then you're getting fuck all."

'I saw Adrian and said to him, "Tell Viv he's getting fuck all and that I'm standing by you."

'At the time, the club was in trouble anyway – it had lost its drinks licence – and he wanted 15 grand out of a club that wasn't making anything.

'A couple of nights after that we went down to the Lion pub in Gateshead. It was a Bank Holiday Monday. Viv was coming out of the Lion as we were going in and there was a little bit of animosity in the air, you could feel it, and we were having a bit of an eye-to-eye.

'Viv said, "Are you all right?"

'I went, "Aye, I'm all right."

'He left a message that he was coming back that night. He was going to come up to the Malting House pub, just up the road from the Lion, but he never turned up. So we'll never know what might have happened.'

7
AN EMPTY MFI UNIT

To the typical thug in the street or everyday villain, Viv was a hardened underworld figure, but to others he was a saviour. Newcastle's John Davison has good reason to remember the generous side of the man. 'I first started boxing as an amateur when I was 25,' he explains. 'I had nothing else to do. I had just got married, I was living in a flat at Throckley in Newcastle and I had bought an MFI unit.

'I had nothing to put on it, a couple of lads said, "Come to the gym in the West End."

'I said, "It's a mug's game!"

'They persisted and said, "Come down, come down."

'So I went down and started punching the bag and Phil Fowler [the coach] said, "Who do you box for?"

'I told him I hadn't boxed and he said, "You have!"

'I replied, "No, I haven't."

'I did some sparring with the lads and knocked three of

them out. They just went crazy and I was told I should be a boxer. Again, I said it was a mug's game. Then again, I had this MFI unit with nothing to fill it, so I thought, I might as well box just to get a few trophies for the unit.

'After the first year I fought the world number one, a boxer called Paul Hodgkinson, an amateur, a great lad. In my first nine fights I had nine knockouts! They stuck me in the ABA national championship at featherweight. I knocked out Paul Hodgkinson in the first round and then I went on to captain England 17 times all over the world.

'Then I was picked for the Olympics and I trained for two years. Politics started to come into it, though. I had already fought a boxer called Michael Delaney and I beat him twice, but they sent him to the Olympics instead of me. There is a long story behind that: they just thought I was too aggressive; I'm more of an aggressive style, more of a professional style. When you box for England, they like a tippy-tappy boxer, jab and move. They don't go a lot for aggression and mine was a very aggressive style, so they didn't go along with that; amateurs don't really like that.

'I won a silver medal against the world number two, Yuri Alexandrov, from Russia, so I naturally thought I was going to the Olympics and I wouldn't have turned pro. I was never at home; every weekend I was always training at Crystal Palace [in London]. It creased the wife when I was overlooked for the Olympics and Delaney was chosen instead, a man I had beaten twice!

'Delaney got beaten in his first fight at the Olympics. To many, he didn't really seem to try; his heart wasn't in it by the look of it. I thought, I'm not going to box amateur any more. Kevin, the national coach, kept phoning me up, asking me to stay on as an amateur, but it didn't change my mind.

'How Viv came into it was that, when I turned professional, I was looking for a sponsor and I was looking all over and somebody mentioned Viv's name. I asked him if he knew anybody who would sponsor me. Viv offered to sponsor me to the tune of £1,000, which helped me get all my gym equipment and other items. I had a proper gumshield, gloves, boots, headguard and a gown. Our sparring friendship grew. Viv used to come into the gym and spar with me. He couldn't believe how strong I was for a featherweight.

'Viv must have been around 18 or 20 stone at the time and he could punch, really punch. His hand speed was very fast, he was tremendously fast for a big fellow. Your hand speed is a lot different from your body speed and it was a natural thing he was doing when he was boxing. You train all the time with your hands, that's how you get your hand speed, but with your top-half speed you go with the flow. Hand speed doesn't mean the rest of your body is fast. [This obviously accounts for Viv's ability to be able to sort out two or three men in seconds.]

'Personally speaking, I thought Viv was a great kid, a real nice gentleman. I didn't know anything about his lifestyle. He helped me out, he started me off in boxing; him and Rob Armstrong, they were the ones that gave me the money.

'When Viv was an amateur boxer, he thought about going professional. When we were sparring, I said that with his size and strength he could probably beat half the professionals in the country at that time. I used to say to him, "You want to turn professional."

'I had Viv's name on my gown in the last fight I had when he was alive, as a "thank you" for him giving me that £1,000. I had the words "John Davison, Sponsored by Viv Graham" put on my gown, but the cameras avoided that area and it was covered over. It was just a friendly sort of thing to do, as he gave me the money to get me started off. I suppose he started my career. It might have seemed that I was advertising thuggery, but it was simply returning the favour. The first gloves that I won the world international title with, I'm sure I gave Viv those gloves.

'I was pleased of Viv's help and I was pleased to present his kids with my gown so that they could say, "My dad sponsored John Davison, the first man from Newcastle in 60 years to win two world international titles and a British title."

'Thanks, Viv.'

8
RIDING THE TIGER

Lee Duffy's last long-term girlfriend, Lisa Stockell, says of her man, 'Lee wanted a quieter life than the life he was leading because he had kids and he wanted to settle down. He'd been in prison, he'd done it all and he'd had enough. He wanted to quieten down more instead of the fighting and all of the attempts on his life; he'd had enough of it. That's what I wanted him to do, quieten down and move away, and I felt as long as we were around here that his life would never quieten down because of what he was. I just felt there would be more attempts to kill him, there had already been so many.'

Just as Viv, living in a tough part of Newcastle, wanted to move away to a nice place and have a quiet life, so did his counterpart on Teesside. But neither was to discover contentment.

Lisa continues, 'I remember Lee saying to me, "How do I get out? What do I have to do?"

'The first time Lee was shot was at a blues party; he was

shot in the knee. He drove home and I was in bed. I heard a beeping of a car horn outside and I went to the car. Lee was in the driving seat and he said, "I've been shot!" I didn't believe him at first and then he fell out of the car and I just ran in and got my mam. We drove him to hospital. I didn't think of anything other than getting him to hospital, I didn't have time to be in shock.

'The second attempted murder was at another blues party. They'd come to my house, but I don't want to talk about that part, they then went on to the blues and they caught him inside. It was when he was fighting with them, that's when he was shot in his foot. Lee wouldn't make statements to the police about these things, but this time he told me to make a statement to the police because of what they'd done to me and he said, "Tell them everything." But Lee said nothing to the police and he told me not to worry about it and that he'd sort it himself.

'I wasn't surprised to learn that Lee had other women because that's how I ended up with him. He was only young when I met him and he didn't have a name for himself then; he was only 18 years old and I was only 15. That was when Lee ended up getting his four-year prison sentence in 1988 for having a fight in a nightclub and doing something to someone's eye.

'At that time, Lee had a girlfriend, but at the beginning of his sentence, the relationship with her ended completely, so then I helped him through his time and when he came out, we had Kattieleigh, our daughter, and that's when it all started.

'When he was in prison, he trained and trained, but when he was released, he didn't do much training: he did it all in his four-year sentence, which is why he was so big. When he came home, he used to keep fit; he never had a regular thing of going to the gym every day or every week. Maybe now and again he'd go with a friend, but it wasn't a regular thing, but he liked going to the gym and keeping fit.

'He was only out for a year and a half and then he died; everything had happened in that short space of time. I remember we went out for a meal with the Sayers, but I wasn't aware that they were a crime family and I wasn't aware of a fight going to take place between Viv Graham and Lee until after Lee's death. When Lee wasn't home he was completely different.

'We lived with my mam for a while because we didn't have our own house and he'd come in and bathe Kattieleigh, take her out and do things. Lee was a family man and there was a really nice side to him. We'd take the kids out, including those from his previous relationship, to the park and do things together like a family.

'I never ever knew Lee dealt in drugs until it was said in the newspapers; they said he was bullying this one and that one, but when I was with him he was never bullying. The only time I've ever known him to fight with people was with drug dealers and they've always made attempts [at murder] on him. I've never known Lee go out and pick a fight on someone innocent.

'When threats started coming, Lee moved out of my mam's house because he didn't want our lives to be in danger any more. We'd go and stay at different houses after that, we'd go and stay at friends. I just accepted it, so everywhere Lee went, I went too.

'Even though Lee was threatened, he still went out on the

town, he still took me to Middlesbrough and still went to all the places he went. He never hid anywhere.

'People showed him loads of respect. As soon as he went into a pub, they'd all come over and sit and drink with him and talk with him. The press said that when Lee went into a pub, the place emptied and everybody stopped enjoying themselves, but that just wasn't true.

'Lee went to all the pubs and everybody stayed and had drinks with him and played pool with him. If people didn't want to be in his company then they wouldn't have stayed, but they did. He never drank much, he'd drink more Coke than anything; he wasn't a drinker.

'Once he went drinking in the afternoon and the front door opened … he just fell in. He'd only been out a few hours and he was absolutely legless. All the lads had been drinking and he joined in, but he didn't usually drink.

'Lee never had his own car, he'd borrow a car to get around in. If he needed one then he'd hire a car for a week or so if we were socialising and sometimes he'd go to the races and things like that.

'Lee loved dancing, he loved a joke and he was really generous to his friends and it's not true that he had lots of enemies. The only enemies he had were the people who dealt in drugs.

'When he came home, he switched off and he was good to his kids; he had two children to his ex-girlfriend. We used to go and pick these two up and go out for the rest of the day to Redcar or wherever and then maybe we'd go and visit my dad at Liverpool; he remarried and moved there.

'I remember that Lee once broke down crying; it was at a

time when he was tired and worn out, and he'd had that many attempts on his life and there'd been three this time. I think he needed a rest, but he couldn't rest! He was never ever in fear because he still got up and went out into town after he'd been shot, so he can't have been frightened; he'd just had enough.

'He just felt like he wanted to settle down, but maybe he thought he couldn't with the attempts on my house and the attempts on his life; he'd just had enough. We wanted to settle down, but everything happened so quick, we didn't have time to sit down and talk, we were both young.

'Lee once said to me, "All I want to do is settle down with you and Kattieleigh, that's all I want, get the house together." We'd got this house, and the night before he died, for some reason he just wanted to stay in this house, so we went and stayed here and slept on the bare floorboards.

'Just the week before his death, he was there decorating it, stripping paint, he wanted to do it all from scratch. He had no money, no car, nothing. He didn't even have a wardrobe full of clothes. He used to wear jeans and sweatshirts and his favourite was shorts; he liked to show his legs off, he liked his legs. He'd even go to the nightclub in his shorts.'

The saying 'He who rides the tiger can never dismount' is relevant to both Duffy and Viv's plight. Both were trapped in the violent lifestyle they had chosen, and there was only one way out.

9
WHAT MAKES A MAN TICK?

Y̱ou might think that Viv Graham's fiancée, Anna
Connelly, was privy to all of his little secrets, but she
wasn't. Viv was a complex man with complex problems. He
was forever searching within himself for answers to life's
problems, but he never found them.

Anna met Viv before he had gained his reputation as a hard
man. She takes up the story:

'When I met him in 1986, he didn't have a name and at that
time I was still married, but separated. I was out on the town
in Newcastle with my sisters and the first thing I noticed about
Viv were his lovely teeth.

'Viv was a gentleman in every way, pulling seats out and
opening doors. He was like that with everyone. Someone who
was being nice to me made the difference, as I wasn't used to
that. I remember Viv walking towards me with a big smile on
his face and he said, "Do you ladies want a drink?"

'There was about six of us sitting there. He kept looking over all of the time, so I knew he wasn't going to come over and just ask the time. I wasn't aware that Viv was having a relationship with anyone else at that time. Although he said he had a few ex-girlfriends with kids to him and that he would always see his kids, he was a single free man.

'We kept going for a few weeks, getting drinks off him and then Viv asked me out.

'My sister-in-law went and told my husband that I was seeing Viv, we had a fight and after about five weeks we split up and I went to stay at my mam's. About three weeks after that, Viv found out and he came to see me and said, "You're not seeing your husband now, so will you go out with me on your own without your family?"

'At that time, he had a girl, Jodie Annie, to Julie Rutherford and had one boy, Dean, to Gillian Lowes. I had been in love before, but not in this way. I'll probably not meet anyone again.

'Viv was still close to his children. Viv's parents love their grandchildren and were visited every day by them and Viv called to see them every day. Our relationship didn't interfere with this. He loved his kids; he loved to see them happy. He travelled to see them every day, no matter what.

'At one time, Viv started work as a labourer for John Wilkinson and he started travelling up to see his children at night-time so he could fit the job in. Viv was working on roofs and that helped supplement his income at that time.

'In the beginning, he wasn't really known; the only thing he did was to have a few fights. His name wasn't big then, but as time went on it became bigger. He wasn't a villain, all that he used to do was have a fight.

'If you were in the pub and you were a big lad and were being cheeky and the manager said, "This man is being cheeky here," then Viv would come across and say, "Look, will you please leave the bar and stop causing trouble."

'He didn't come across and cause you trouble or beat you up. He would ask you a few times and, if you didn't leave, he would then hit you and knock you out. He didn't like picking things up and hitting you with it. When he hit them, he used to catch them before they fell and take them outside and wait with them until they came around and sent them on their way by saying, "Son, don't come back. I've asked you three times and then you wouldn't leave," and that was Viv. He wasn't a rotter like the West End lot, hitting you with anything, punching you all over and then kicking you down the stairs! Viv wouldn't dream of anything like that. People came for him to sort out the bother; he never ever asked them. People came to the door to ask him to go and sort trouble out in the bars, saying that the police had sent them.

'I had a marvellous lifestyle; I bought dresses and things from Peaches & Cream [a Newcastle clothes shop, now closed, with an elite clientele]. Viv would buy me dresses valued at £600 and £700. He would spend £1,000 on a dress and shoes to match.

'Whatever I liked, he would buy it for me and that pleased him. As long as it made me happy, then he was happy. He liked to give things, but he didn't like them if they were short dresses! He would buy them and then, when he got home, if he didn't like them, he wouldn't speak to you because they would be too revealing.

'He would say, "Have you seen how short that dress is?"

'I would say, "What did you buy it for then? You made me try it on in the shop!"

'Then we would start arguing and then the dress would get ripped up and that was the end of that. My mam would say, "What have you paid all that money for?"

'Viv would reply, "Well, Irene, it's bad enough being in the town watching your own back without lads looking at your lass with short frocks on – it just makes matters worse!"

'I said to my mother, "He just wants me to wear polo necks and long skirts."

'I didn't want to wear them because I was only in my twenties.

'He underestimated himself all of the time, and he was a bundle of nerves and his stomach used to turn over, and he'd end up sitting on the toilet.

'He was never like, "I'm Viv Graham, don't mess with me!" He didn't have loads of confidence. If he ever lost a bit of weight, he would think he was too small. He was never six foot-odd tall, yet his father was. Viv was only five foot eleven inches tall.

'He would be worried if he got involved in a fight with a gang! Viv never had loads of confidence and he loved to be really big and, if he looked in the mirror and he was really big, then he was happy.

'It was because of his name really, but he never used to be that big when he boxed, as his weight was only 13 stone. He could do the same when he was big as he could do at 13 stone; he was actually fitter.

'Then he got into the body-building stuff and he went even bigger! He got involved because a lot of his friends were doing that and eating the tuna and chicken. When he was in the gym, it was one against the other; he didn't want to be fat, though.

'He went to the gym two or three times a day and he did once try steroids by injection, but he took bad with them and he ended up with an abscess on his backside and needed an operation. He was frightened of needles. I said, "I'm telling your dad on you."

'He used to get in bad tempers, but he never touched the kids or me. He used to pull the doors off, but I wasn't bothered because he used to replace them the next day.

'The confidence he lacked, the steroids gave him. He couldn't ever get the confidence because he wasn't an aggressive man. He couldn't get into a bad temper easily. It used to take him a long time to get like that. People used to worry, thinking he was getting softer. When he was supposed to do things, he couldn't get the aggression there. But, with steroids, the aggression came straight away, but then that wasn't him.

'He knew where the aggression was coming from [steroids] and he decided himself to come off them because his dad said, "You don't need steroids, son. You're a big lad."

'Viv was disciplined because of the boxing he started when he was 13 years old, and he did that right up until he was in his twenties. Most people that ever met him knew that he was a gentleman and very soft-hearted. He could easily cry over his nanna's memories. He always had a wreath at Christmas to put on her grave.

'Viv used to give me chocolates and flowers as a romantic gift, but he never wrote me any poetry, as he wasn't a good writer ... but he could write a bet out, no problem.

'He used to nip into town and get me make-up and lipstick and buy me nice underwear. He went into that shop called Secrets, regardless of his size and being well known. It never bothered him a little bit and, if I ran out of a lipstick, then I would say, "Oh! My make-up!"

'He'd say, "Where's it from?"

'I would reply, "Fenwicks."

Straight away, he'd run there. If I wanted stockings, he'd ask, "What colour do you want?"

'If I wanted lipsticks, he got me ten lipsticks. Viv and his friend, Alan Rooney, who was with him every single day, went for the make-up.

'Alan was later charged with blackmail because of something he got involved with and it was traced back to Alan because his child had picked the telephone up and said, "Hello?"

That's how he got caught in a blackmail plot when he had threatened a publican's husband with Viv, because the man had used Viv's name in vain. This other man was using Viv's name, but Alan ended up getting eight years behind bars for something stupid like that.

[Blackmail is a filthy, heinous crime, but in Alan Rooney's case it would seem that the word 'blackmail' should be changed to 'demanding money with menaces'. If you play with fire, you get burned.

'Alan was just out of hospital after that, having had some sort of virus; he was really bad with it. It took over his whole body and, you know when you see someone with multiple sclerosis, he was just like that for months and months.

'Alan was at our house every day, but Viv had been told

when he was in the town that this man [the one that Rooney blackmailed] had not been using his true name. Alan had no money and said, "Should I phone him up and say whatever?"

'Viv said, "Do what you want."

'I think he [Rooney] said, "I'll burn your house down."

'He had no intention of doing it.

'Before Alan had done all this, Viv and I had gone to that man once and he had given Viv money for something he had done. From then on, he thought he was well in with Viv, sort of thing, "I've given Viv a bit job and paid him some money, me and Viv are like that."

'When Viv died, the man wouldn't drop the charges against Alan. If Viv had still been alive, things might have turned our very differently.

'When Viv lost his driving licence for 12 months, Alan was the one to drive him around. That was another story. Viv went to pick the kids up and this woman stepped straight off the kerb and he bumped into her; luckily she wasn't hurt.

'I went straight to the scene and found her there with broken glasses. A couple living opposite had seen it happen and phoned me up. Viv was absolutely devastated!

'Viv gave her £200 to replace the broken glasses. We went to the flower shop and got a big bouquet of flowers for her, found out where she lived and went back to the house with the flowers and gave her another £100. Her husband was there when this took place.

'Within six weeks she took a private summons out against Viv and got him done. As it happened, his car wasn't insured. She said she was getting severe headaches, but, when she issued a private summons and the police wanted Viv's documents, he wasn't insured and he lost his licence. The little old lady still carried on with the private summons. Viv died before it reached court.

'Viv was genuinely sick over it. He gave her that money and was worried about her regardless of the insurance, as he did not know his insurance had expired. That will show you what type of a person Viv was.

'When people asked Viv to do them a favour, he always had respect for the elderly and many a time he turned down a job if the person he had to go and see was old. Many a time, though, he didn't really have to do anything. A lot of businessmen came to him. Say, for instance, you had fitted windows to a house and you knew you weren't going to get the money, you would go to Viv for help to get it. Then the money would be there the next day when Viv called to collect it.

'Some of the things said about Viv were all lies, things like he was a big drug baron! He never ever dealt in drugs! That was one thing he never ever touched. He never needed to deal in drugs; he made a lot of money from other things. He had bars and nightclubs [supervising the doors and troubleshooting for breweries] from Whitley Bay through to Wallsend and Shields Road, into the town [Newcastle city centre].

'Some weeks he picked up maybe £15,000, that was apart from businessmen and other people knocking at the door. I was there when Viv had to collect £60,000 and he got £30,000 in a carrier bag; he never needed to touch drugs. People just accepted what was put out about him; no one would stand up and defend him when he passed away.

'Viv never thought of what he could do with his money. He

did at the finish with this house, but before that he wasn't interested, he just liked to spend it; he didn't drink and he didn't smoke … he just liked a bet. Viv could have bought the house outright, he could have bought his car outright, but he got it all on finance. After Viv's death, his dad paid for his car every week.

'He liked it better that way, getting the house on a mortgage. He didn't have a penny put to one side for emergencies! As quick as it came in, the quicker it went out. He could have had £30,000 in that hand and within an hour he wouldn't have £1 for the electric meter! It never bothered him; he knew, if he spent it by the Monday, he would have more by the weekend. Tomorrow didn't matter, he lived for the day and I was just the same.

'At times it was a competition to see who could win the most money. Every day we were in the bookies, he would say, "There's your money." I would put a bet on and say, "Give me £100 so I can put this bet on." I would maybe win, because I was luckier than he was.

'I still put the odd bet on now. I had done that prior to meeting Viv. We bought a greyhound and it cost us a fortune, it didn't come anywhere in the races it ran in, but we could watch it in the races and have a night out. We even thought about buying a racehorse, but that's as far as it went.

'We had 32 rabbits, 2 geese, 5 dogs and 36 chickens and they took a lot of looking after. Viv loved the chickens and collecting the eggs in the morning. Although Viv ate chicken for his meals when he trained, he wouldn't have been able to eat one of these chickens for Sunday dinner. He went shooting with his dad, but he couldn't have shot anything we had just for the sake of eating it. He shot at pheasants in the wild on these shoots, but that was it.

'Viv and I didn't lead a boring life; we went to the best of restaurants and everything. Viv didn't like paying his debts, although he did pay up in the end. If we got anything on HP, it would end up not getting paid for, so we used to buy things outright. A television man knocked on the door and Viv wouldn't pay him. When he saw it was Viv, he didn't come back. The poll-tax man came and he saw Viv and asked who he was and I just said something like, "He's my brother." We were all laughing.

'Viv said, "You'll get no money from here!"

'The man said, "I'm away, me." He didn't come back.

'He loved life and he was up at six o'clock in the morning with the dogs. He was even happier when we got [our dog] Buster. There was a big field at the back and he was looking forward to getting up and running, because he loved training. He used to make me get up with him and wanted me to run around the field with him! I still had my pyjamas on and used to walk around the field with the dogs. The neighbour next door used to laugh when he saw me out with him.

'Viv didn't like me smoking because he didn't, so he limited me to ten cigarettes a day, but I had my secret supply hidden. I used to keep the same packet and top it up. He would say, "You've only had two tabs today!"

'Although Viv went into an environment where there was cigarette smoke, he didn't like me smoking because it was bad for my health. He couldn't stand the smell of the smoke and he used to get bathed and showered two or three times a day. Every time he came back from the gym or from somewhere smelly, he would have a shower. We had someone come in and help out with the cleaning, so we didn't have a big pile of ironing building up in the corner.

'As for Viv's safety, he confided in me about this and many a time raised his concerns about him or I being shot. He used to say all the time, "I'll never reach 40 because, I'm telling you, they'll shoot me."

'I thought he was invincible and nothing could happen to him. I just thought when he said it, that they would be too frightened to come and they wouldn't try it.

'A gang of masked men came to my house when I lived in Daisy Hill at Wallsend and the windows came in! There were two carloads of them and they had masks on and were carrying guns! Viv didn't hide from anyone and his telephone number was available from the directory.

'We used to go on holiday and our favourite place was Greece. I would see a different Viv. We never ever went where it was lively; sometimes we were the only people on the beach. We would come back, get changed and go for a meal. We didn't ever go to Tenerife, though, as it was reported that Viv had been there and had a fight with a man called Andy Winder. People said that Winder did timeshare in Tenerife.

'I remember, Paddy Leonard wanted Viv to come across and do the timeshare. Viv's dad said, "No way!"

'There are things coming out these last few years that even I didn't know about because I was so high on Valium! In all of that time there are things I am just starting to question now.

'When we went on holiday, we went there as a family and we didn't want to come back. We wanted it to last for ever and wanted to move away, but we said we'd just stay here for a few years. He loved the country and he wanted to be away, but his work was here and he was becoming more established. Half the time he didn't even have to show his face: he had the likes of Rob Armstrong and them in nightclubs overseeing it for him.

'Viv was going to get contracts on the books and do it properly; some jobs could pay £1,000 a week. That was happening just before he died. It was all coming together, he was going to give the town up and leave it at that. He was sick of having to put his face up against it all of the time. People wanted to use Viv's name above their doors.

'With regards to Higgins Security, they came from Birmingham and asked Viv to visit them there and meet their top bosses. Viv told his dad and he was told not to go there and to make them come here to meet him. They told Viv they didn't want to take over the town because they knew he was *Viv Graham*.

'A lot of the doormen were complaining because they feared Higgins were coming here to Newcastle and taking their jobs and they were saying to Viv, "You'll have to stop them because they're taking our jobs! You'll have to show them!"

'They knew all about Viv and he went to see them and they said they had no intention of taking over the bars. Viv sorted that entire lot out for them.

'Viv hated me wearing short skirts and sometimes he went overboard. I remember once when we were out, off he went to the toilet through a crowd of women and he would keep his hands in the air. If he saw anyone touch a woman and the woman complained, he didn't take kindly to that happening, especially if it was to me.

'I remember once when someone was talking to me, Viv went across and said, "That was my wife!" They didn't do it again.

'When I first met Viv, he was with me constantly, but sometimes there would be one night when he wouldn't be there and the next day I would say, "Where were you?"

'He would tell me a pack of lies and say, "Oh, I was in the casino in the town until seven o'clock this morning, I had my breakfast." Which was a load of crap!

'Viv's best quality was his kindness; if he had a fault then it was being overly generous. People would call, crying to the door, saying they had a gas bill. He would pull the money out and give it to them, but he never got it back from them.

'I don't think Viv was trying to overcompensate because he was a non-believer. I was a good Catholic. Viv's funeral was in a Protestant church, although he wasn't a believer in God and had no intention of accepting my faith, so he had no reason to want to prove something.

'I believe he started to believe in God more, although his father was a staunch non-believer. I think it was because Viv got on well with Father Conaty and the fact that missionaries from Bosnia started coming to our house when we put them up. It was through me that Viv started to change his views.

'I remember it was the first Holy Communion of one of my daughters and the table was full of religious gifts; he bought the full whack for all the kids there. Once you met him, you never forgot him and I used to say to the Father that Viv was something special, because he *was* somebody special to me.

'I couldn't believe how very kind in his ways he was and yet still have this power inside of him. He was very strong; he could push out a 580-pound bench-press, not a problem to him. He gave a lot of help to the local boxing club and had the heating put in and did a lot more. Viv paid for everything.

'We had our arguments, just like anybody else. Viv would come back from the gym, lie on the settee, have loads of sweets and watch videotapes. That's what he liked the most; he would lock the door and take the phone off the hook.

'As for children, I didn't think we needed a child to cement our relationship and Viv didn't because I had my children and he had his children, but then there came a point when he did. We did try, but it just never happened. I went to the doctor and put a pregnancy test in and I was frightened to say the real results after the way Viv went on.

'We came out of the surgery and I told him I was pregnant and he jumped for joy and wanted to tell everyone. We rushed back home and he was starting to telephone his mother. I put the receiver down and said, "I've got something to tell you."

'I was frightened after the way he went on. I thought, Eh, why did I say that to him?

'I said, "I was only pretending."

'He went, "You what!"

'I said, "I just pretended to you, just to see what you would think."

'He was gutted, really gutted, and then I realised he really did want a baby.

'I was frightened in case I had one, as he wouldn't love my kids in the same way. We did want one then, this was about three months before he died, so we did start and try. He loved them and they loved him and they even called him their dad. He spent more time with them than he did with his own kids.

'I was from a mixed family and I knew there might be

problems, as I had some problems in my family, although they weren't problems of a bad nature. Because I had the experience from that I thought that Viv might encounter some problems with that scenario.

'Viv said, "I would treat them exactly the same."

'I said, "Other people's are never the same as your own. Your two come here and I love them, but I don't love them as I love my own."

'So I knew, if I had ever had a baby, then that love would have been a special love, different to the love he would have for them.

'This would have caused arguments and I didn't want that because we had a happy relationship. I didn't want that. I didn't want to start fighting. I knew he really did want a baby and we did try. My children said, "We can have a little baby sister or a baby brother."

'They [Anna's two daughters: Dominique and Georgia] talk about him every day. They've got their pictures in their rooms and they talk about him all the time. They absolutely loved him. She [Dominique] has got her own little book that she makes her own little poems in. The kids put the monkey hanging on the rear-view mirror that was in Viv's car and he just left it there.

'Sometimes Viv's business and private life overlapped. He would call me and come and get something to eat, then he would go straight back out to the gym and from there on to the bookies. He would come out, go for something to eat and go and get some videos, then, seven o'clock, he would ask us if we wanted anything from the shop.

'He would watch a video with his bag of sweets, with the

phone off the hook and the door locked. If something cropped up, which usually it did, he would take me with him and I would sit in the car waiting. My sister, Mary, and him were very close; she would stand up to anybody, even a man!

'Just after I had lost Viv, there was further tragedy when my brother-in-law, Harry Thompson, was tragically lost to violence. Mary's husband had gone to sort out someone who had burgled his home and he was stabbed. I couldn't believe it. He died about nine months after Viv. I was just starting to get back on my feet. I couldn't believe it; I just couldn't believe it.

'I remember a particular incident when a ship had pulled into the Tyne and the sailors were causing bother. One of them was a championship boxer, about six foot ten tall. He touched a woman's behind. Viv said, "Here, you wouldn't do that where you come from, so you won't do that here in Newcastle, touching lasses' backsides!"

'So he [the sailor] took his sunglasses off and said to Viv, "Who are you, man?"

'Viv said, "Never mind who I am!"

'He [the sailor] just went *bop!* Viv's tooth went through his lip. Anyway, Viv banged him and the sailor went down. The police were sitting in their car watching it. They said they saw the big black man and stood up for Viv, as a lot of the police liked Viv. Viv got away with that one.

'Where we used to live was terrible! There was crack and heroin! You could go and knock on any door and get it. When the football club was there, Viv would take about 50 kids on the field and he would say, "Don't take drugs, get training."

'Kids loved him, and if they could get into the car with him it made their day. I knew all the hard men you could think of or name and Viv was nothing like that.

'If Viv hit you, he wouldn't let you fall in case you hit your head on the ground. Viv never took liberties with people, yet others did and they are all still alive. Viv first started in Wheelers nightclub and he had trouble with a Gateshead man called Paul Ashton, now serving 31 years for violence!

'Viv wouldn't use his power against someone weighing only about eight or nine stone; he would pull his punch back. Viv gave Stevie "The Hammer" Eastman a nasty bash! I was there when it happened. I didn't like fighting but it wasn't as if it was a fight that would last for ages. Viv was as fast as lightning!

'If you were a big person, he would give a harder punch. He wouldn't punch a man of eight stone the way he punched Stevie, because it would have punched their face in. After all of that, Stevie didn't hold any grudge against Viv. He thought the world of Viv and they still remained friends even though that happened, and Viv thought a lot of Stevie.

'Every New Year, the press would phone me, even at ten o'clock at night. They phoned me up one day. I had been going to the spiritualist, I didn't know where I was at that time and I felt that I needed it.

'They tripped me up by pretending to be someone I knew. [The Catholic Church condemns spiritualism, regarding it as necromancy, contacting the dead.] A woman rung me up and said, "How are you? Have you had any more messages from the spiritualist, have you? Were you there on Sunday?"

'There am I, blabbing away, because I didn't really know who it was. I said, "Yes, I got a message." I was telling her the full message and by the end of the conversation I still couldn't work out who it was and I said, "Who is it, anyway?" That weekend it was plastered all over the newspapers.

'The police called about this Blackpool thing where a lad, Gary Ward, was charged with the murder of a man, Mark White, on Blackpool beach. Viv had never ever been to Blackpool, never, ever.

'It just so happened, that month being September and my birthday is 1 September, he definitely wasn't there. I wonder where Viv Graham comes into it. I wish that woman [Gary Ward's mother] had come to me. I would have said that no way was Viv there. The police said the man [Gary Ward] was 18 years old and fighting Viv on the beach. He wouldn't have had a chance with Viv.

'Look at Stephen Craven, who was sent to prison over the Studio nightclub [in Newcastle] murder of Penny Laing. It was supposed to be another man and that man went to London. Viv phoned the man up and told him to come back. He was in the Marines or something and the doorman at the Studio nightclub was alleged to have let him out of the side door. Viv had a confrontation with the doorman who supposedly did that and, eventually, Viv ended up being good friends with Stephen Craven.

'Every night I go to bed and I can't sleep very well. I might sleep maybe about two and a half to three hours. I must be in a deep sleep, because by the next day I'm fit enough and not worn out. I'm always on the go, so that must be all I need. Before Viv died, you couldn't get me out of the bed, I could sleep and sleep and sleep.

'Viv's views on someone who committed crimes against old people were what you would expect from someone like him.

Viv had no proper friends except for those in my family who were really close to him. Since he died, I can say he has no friends. No one has given me any support that could be looked at as anything real.

'I would like to mention Robbie Warton; he was a good true friend to the children.

'Also, Rob Bell has helped; they were very good to Viv's family, but the rest of them just used him. Rob Bell nearly died when he was attacked in Newcastle on a night out in the Bigg Market. It was because of an argument where words were exchanged that inflamed those involved.

'They went to Santino's restaurant; it was a night out on the spur of the moment. Some men walked in with the gun towards where Viv and Rob were sitting. Viv said, "Put that gun away before I shove it up your arse." Viv grabbed the gun and then they went outside. After a fight, it ended up, allegedly, that Viv broke the jaw of one of Rob's attackers, as Rob lay there nearly bleeding to death after being stabbed in the heart by one of the men.

'It was said that Viv was put into prison for a savage attack on Stuart Watson. Why didn't the newspapers say that the man Viv attacked was 18½ stone? Eventually Viv and Stuart became friends because, after Viv got out of prison, things were said and the air needed clearing, so Viv went to see Stuart and the matter was settled without the use of violence. Viv was invited to parties that Stuart held, so that proves Viv wasn't a thug as the newspapers portrayed him.

'Viv's boxing career led to an involvement with a fellow heavyweight amateur boxer, Manny Burgo, from South Shields. The boxing selectors chose Manny over and above

Viv to go and box for the championships. Viv wasn't very happy at this and Manny said, "Viv, it wasn't my fault." This is what made Viv throw the towel in, as he knew he was a better boxer than Manny, but Manny was chosen because he looked a better boxer. People say it was because of a frozen shoulder that Viv stopped, but that was the real reason. He went back to boxing after that, though, for a while.

'Viv didn't need to live up to people; he liked to be on his own. We were out in Julie's nightclub one night when Viv was involved in a fight and there were loads of them. Viv was fighting with these men and everybody that knew Viv had moved away from him over to the other side, but Tim Healy hadn't! He came up to Viv to pass by and was clipped, but Viv hadn't realised it was Tim Healy and it wasn't until afterwards that they said, "You've hit Tim Healy!" Viv thought that he was going to get the police involved. There was a joke that Pat Roach would be coming in to get Viv. Roach was a real-life professional wrestler who [like Healy] played a part in [BBC TV's] *Auf Wiedersehen, Pet*.

'Viv's hero was his dad and his favourite film was *Zulu*. There was only one man Viv looked up to and that was his dad.

'Viv was a real professional, he looked after you, but, as for himself, he only lived for the day. He didn't put anything to one side for a rainy day. If he had got older and couldn't do that profession any more, then he might have thought about it.

'We did once try to save; we opened a bank account for a mortgage. He gave me £200 to put into the bank and [a few weeks later] I asked for a balance, which was given to me as £2.82.

'I exclaimed, "You had better check it, as that's not right!"

'The clerk said, "Well, how much?"

'I replied, "There's a lot of money in it, you'd better check it."

'So she checked it all and said, "There's definitely only £2.82 left in the account."

'I said, "Well, you'd better get the manager because there's definitely more. I know what I put in!"

'When all came to all, Viv had been going in and signing a piece of paper and getting the money out for the bookies. Another woman came and said, "Your Viv's been coming in and signing the piece of paper and drawing out every week."

'I wasn't bothered. I went back to the bookies and pulled him; he was full of himself, laughing! He knew when I went in what he had done. I said, "You're joking, there's me going in and them saying there's only £2.82, well, that's me finished."

'So I let that one go and I never ever tried to save again. The bankbook is still upstairs with £2.82 in.

'My brother, my sister and her husband loaned me the £12,000 as a deposit on this house. We didn't ever get to pay the mortgage, as Viv died. There was an insurance policy that covered it, but it wasn't paid out because it was in probate because [Viv's former girlfriend] Gillian Lowes is contesting it.

[Since then, the insurance payout has been settled and all concerned have received some sort of payment.]

'Viv wasn't a gangster, as such. The gangsters we know are underground London types, where they put people into cement bridges and that sort of thing. Viv wasn't that type of man; he was a boxer and he could handle himself. The people that knew him loved him. He was an absolute gentleman. The people that hadn't really heard about him thought that he only did nasty things. They just thought, Ugh! Viv Graham, he's a rotter! But, if they really knew him, they would have felt completely different.

'People knew what he was capable of and he didn't use a weapon. They knew he would come face to face with them and what they didn't know was that he would always give them a chance. He wouldn't just run, he would say to them, "Look, don't do that, don't be like ..." and, if he got another phone call about them, then they were in bother, but he would let them walk away.

'One Saturday afternoon we were going for a meal and we bumped into a man Viv knew; he was called Durant. We were out on a Saturday afternoon shopping and going for a meal when Durant stopped us and took his coat off and said to Viv, "I can't work anywhere, you stopped me from working. I've got a mortgage!"

'Viv said, "Me? Not me! I wouldn't stop you working anywhere."

'Durant then said, "I've had enough."

'Viv said to the man's wife, "Tell your man to put his coat back on."

'Viv was on parole, he'd just got out of jail and he didn't want to have a fight and he wouldn't. They had a scuffle, the lad fell off the kerb and Viv picked him up and gave him £50 and said, "I'll give you a job any time."

'It was Rob Armstrong that he had had a fight with, not Viv, but the rumour was that Viv wouldn't let Durant work on any of the doors in the town.

'A fight between Durant and Rob Armstrong sometime, months earlier, in Madison's nightclub had resulted in some damage being caused to this man's eye. Viv was being blamed for it, but it wasn't him who did it.

'Then there was John Jobie from Gateshead. He had started carrying a lot of tales and he came into Julie's nightclub with his wife. Viv went up to him and he said to Viv, "It was a load of lies."

'He said to Viv, "I'll go with you to their doors and prove they are lying."

'Viv said to me, "Anna, what do you think? Do you think it's rumours?"

'I replied, "They will be rumours, because people like to start trouble. You know what people are like."

'I used to believe them, but the rumour was that John Jobie wanted Viv seeing to. Viv didn't believe it and I didn't believe it either. That's how trouble started, but this ended up in a friendly manner and Viv was still friends with John Jobie.

'I recall Viv being pally with Dodgy Ray Hewitson. He was one of Viv's closest friends, but they fell out.

'The man who cradled the dying Viv, Terry Scott, he was a friend of Viv's, but I wouldn't say he was one of his best friends.'

10
HAREM NIGHTS AND FIGHTS

Just as Lee Duffy had an abundance of love in his short life, so did Viv Graham. Three main women, and more besides, featured in Viv's tangled love life. After his death, these three women who made up Viv's 'harem'– Julie Rutherford, Gillian Lowes and Anna Connelly – were involved in a long and torturous struggle to gain a share in the proceeds of insurance payouts.

There was no other woman in Viv's life – just other women!

Viv used to call Gillian 'Little Lowesy'. When they were at school, they had pet names for each other. Years later Viv used to call at Gillian's home and complain of terrible headaches, having gone there directly from Anna's. Gillian put these headaches down to pressure and not to the boxing, which some people thought was the cause.

She said it was the job that Viv was doing that was the cause of the stress. Everybody wanted looking after by him, she said, and it really got out of hand so that in the end he could not cope.

'In the last year of his life,' Gillian said, 'he was receiving lots of threats and he was really stressed out.'

Viv did take these threats seriously, she added, and she assumed that someone rang Viv from London to say they were coming up to Newcastle. In fact, Viv did confide in Gillian about this threat he received from London and he said that she had to stop taking the Pill if he received such a threat. It is difficult to tell if this threat was something Viv had invented just to get Gillian off the Pill because he wanted her to have his baby. He liked it if his women were pregnant, as it made them unattractive to other men, and perhaps this was the reason he wanted Anna to try for a baby with him. Maybe that was it: all the outward machismo had made him feel emotionally stunted within, and who could he trust?

Then again, the headaches may just have been another ploy to get Gillian to stop taking the Pill so that he could get her pregnant. Whatever the truth, Viv did ask her to come off the Pill, and that, to Gillian, meant he had received a certain threat he was waiting for. But she still told him he had 'no chance' of her coming off the Pill for him.

If Viv really loved her so much, why did he use every male trick in the book to ditch Gillian when he was invited to go abroad? There was one occasion when they planned to go to Cyprus for a break, Viv having been nominated to be best man at a friend's wedding there. But, when Viv told Gillian that he did not like going abroad, the trip was scrapped.

To make up for this, Gillian booked a holiday on her own in Corfu. When Viv found out, he tried to dissuade her from going, but ended up taking her to the bus station so she could get to the airport. Was this to make sure she was going on her own? A few weeks later, and without Gillian, Viv went off on a holiday abroad.

A place that Viv seemed to enjoy taking his conquests to was Blackpool. He took Gillian and another couple there, and as soon as they arrived Viv was off to the betting shop with the other man in tow. So desperate was Viv to get away and have a bet, he didn't even stay to help get the suitcases out of the car.

The other woman whispered to Gillian that Viv had won a lot of money. Viv denied he had won anything at all. Gillian recalled, however, that she patted his pockets, looking for the money, and the next day found about £500 hidden in a cushion. She went mad at him. If Viv had thought more of his women, surely he would have flashed his cash? Clearly, Gillian did not believe Viv when he said he had not won any money. The difference between Viv and Gillian, which she admits, is that he did not value money.

At the time Gillian was having Viv's first child, he was off seeing Julie Rutherford. Gillian did not want to become pregnant, but she came off the Pill anyway after deciding she no longer needed to take it because their relationship was at an end. But, even though they were no longer together, she and Viv started having sex again. The result was that she became pregnant and had a baby son, Dean.

Viv said to Gillian that he would not live with her but would come home when it was all over. What was he waiting for to be all over? Gillian did not expand on this, but her talking about it suggested she had an idea of what it was.

Viv told Gillian that he did not love Anna Connelly the way he loved her and that she would always be his childhood sweetheart.

Gillian recalled Viv coming back from one of his holidays. 'It was about six o'clock in the morning when he called with a suitcase with three bottles of perfume in it. He said that one bottle was for his mother, but his mother did not ever get it, so it was obvious he had bought each one of his three lovers the same bottle of perfume home from the holiday!'

During that visit, Viv proposed marriage to Gillian and she wrote down his words so as to confirm what he had said. But it was not to be, and she was kept hanging on, as were the other two women.

Viv went off with Julie while he was still seeing Gillian, who was gutted to lose him to another woman. Gillian must have felt second best to Julie, as Julie must have felt second best to Anna when Viv moved on to her, leaving Gillian third best.

Julie was very attracted to Viv when they first met, in Finnigan's bar in Gateshead. Gillian noticed this and became very jealous. Viv was promptly thrown out, along with his eight carrier bags of belongings. He stayed at Gillian's only a few nights of the week as he was still living with his parents then.

Viv took both Gillian and Julie to Blackpool, but for some reason he never took Anna. There was no love lost between her and Gillian. Julie recalls, 'it was before he went to prison in about the March or May of 1989, and that was supposed to be a new beginning and we were sitting in a pub called the Manchester Bar.

'He said, "Whatever happens in the future doesn't count, doesn't matter."

'I had had a few halves and he didn't drink and I asked, "What are you talking about?"

'He again said, "Whatever happens in the future doesn't count, this is a new beginning from today," and he would go on like that.

'I was going, "Yeah, yeah, yeah, right."

'Little did I know at that time that he had been with Gill and obviously she was pregnant and he didn't have the bottle to tell me. I didn't have a clue and then I think we fell out in the September for a while and he was going away on holiday. He said he was going away on business and we ended up having a big huge fight and he went.

'My friend was there and she had seen it all. He was on the phone to her from the airport and whinging on and then he was ringing me, saying that he had made a mistake and this and the other, and he came back. It was just before my birthday, in the September. He was sitting in front of the house, looking up. I was in a different house then. I looked out and thought, What's the matter with him?

'Because he used to come up and confess, I didn't want to hear things. He had come to confess; he said he had actually been away with Anna. It took him about two hours to tell me it all.

'I said, "Just tell me!"

'Viv replied, "No, because you'll leave me. Tell me you won't leave me."

'He wanted me to swear on my bairn's life that I wouldn't leave him.

'I prised it out of him. "Come on, you obviously have something to tell me."

'He half confessed, "You've already just said her name!"

'I just said, "Anna."

'And he went, "Yeah."

'I flipped!

'Then, a couple of days later, it was my birthday and it was crawly, crawly time. I went out on my birthday and he was locked up [in prison] that night, 29 September. He was actually locked up after twelve that night, because we had been out; he dropped me off, went to work and was locked up from there.

'Then, in December, he hit me with the news that "Gill had a baby". Prison visits are about 20 minutes, half an hour, or something. I think I made a lot of enemies at that particular time. People would come on the visit with me and I didn't want them on the visit because I needed to know what, where, who, why, how and everything. I think I was nasty to one or two people and after that I stopped going.

'I said, "That is it!"

'I wasn't getting anywhere. I phoned Rob Armstrong's wife and I said, "Will you tell Viv I won't be back, we're finished?"

'She went, "OK."

'I literally moved house and everything, but then he started to phone. When I went back, he said that Anna had been visiting and he told her that he wanted me to come back in to see him. By this time, it was about March. I had stopped going for weeks and weeks. I used to go about four or five times a week. I know his dad used to go on a Thursday and I would go most other times.'

From what Julie says, it is quite clear that Viv was replacing the loss of Anna's prison visits with Julie's, as Anna said she had walked out during a visit, leaving Viv with the engagement ring. Viv threatened to destroy the prison! Obviously he had a rethink and persuaded Julie to come back.

There were arguments over the paternity of Viv's second child by Julie. By coincidence, after Viv died, Julie and Gillian were attending a solicitor's appointment in connection with his estate, and they spoke briefly. Julie was not comfortable with some things that Gillian related to her and later, in an interview, she felt the need to put her side of the story.

Anna Connelly maintained that for Julie to have become pregnant by Viv (with her second child to him) she would have had to have sex with him while visiting him when he was serving three years for his part in the assault on fellow club doorman Stuart Watson.

Julie says, 'It's true.' She did have sex with Viv while on a prison visit and conceived their second child, Callum. Further discussions on who was Callum's biological father continued:

Julie said, 'The man was Viv's very good friend. There used to be two guys. One used to take me up to see Viv, but he used to aggravate things because Viv was very, very jealous and he used to say stupid things to wind him up. Anything would wind Viv up. "I saw her knickers when she was getting into the car," and that was it!

'So Viv had said, "I don't want him to bring you in any more," because he was a wind-up and other reasons.

'Viv had this other man bring me in, as he had Viv's car at times. I know that Viv had been told that the car had been seen outside my door at six o'clock in the morning, which was a load of rubbish as this man was petrified of Viv. The man that Viv's friend had said was at my house while Viv was in prison wouldn't even look at me from across the road. Who in their right mind would? Who would do it? Would I do it? Be stupid enough to get pregnant by somebody else and face the wrath? No! I don't think so, that's silly,' said Julie, her voice drying up with emotion.

'Viv was not normally violent at home, but,' she replied, 'I think it would be a different kettle of fish if I had told him that I was going with somebody behind his back! Viv was a very, very jealous and possessive man. I don't think he would have taken it lightly.

'I didn't understand why he wasn't at Viv's funeral. Somebody had said they had a fall-out. Why did they fall out? I've never seen this man from visiting prison and I still don't know why they fell out.

When Gillian Lowes was engaged to Viv, everything was fine until she discovered he was seeing Julie Rutherford and she then gave Viv his engagement ring back. This scenario is uncannily like the one in which his last fiancée, Anna Connelly, allegedly returned his engagement ring on a prison visit after she discovered that he was seeing Gillian behind her back and that he was the father of Gillian's latest child.

This so much incensed Anna that she walked out of the visit and did not go back. In fact, it was Viv who went, cap in hand, back to Anna to beg her forgiveness and dedicate himself to being loyal to her once more.

Anna said of this, 'Eventually I caught him out when he went to jail and one of the other two, Gillian Lowes, was pregnant. By this time we had just got engaged and just come back from our holiday. I had found out when she had come to jail to visit and someone I knew had seen her on that visit and they told me she was pregnant.

'I pulled Viv and said that Gillian was pregnant and Viv told me that she had got herself a man. He still wouldn't say it was him until I found out. I went to the jail and gave him the engagement ring back and I told him, "That was it!"

'He pleaded with me, "Please, listen to me! I'll tell you the story!"

'I said, "No way."

'He said, "You walk out of this jail and I'll smash this jail up!"

'I said, "You best smash this jail up, because I'm away!"

Anna said she gave Viv the engagement ring back, yet she also said they got engaged when Viv came out of prison on Mother's Day. Maybe they became re-engaged.

Anna continued, 'After he came out of the jail, he came to me and said, "Will you come back to me?" He had sent me letters and cards and that. I said to Viv that he was a single man and he could do whatever he wanted and to go with Gillian or to go with Julie and whomever he wanted, but he didn't want this, he wanted me.

'We were going to get married and we got engaged on Mother's Day. I said, if he came back, that would have to be the finish with Julie and Gillian and he couldn't have the one night away here and there because that's not what I wanted. I wanted a proper relationship. He loved my children and they loved him.'

However, right up until the day Viv died, he kept all of his love interests going.

At the time of Viv's spell in prison, Gillian and his family were all friendly and acted like a family by visiting him as a group. Julie, though, stopped visiting, and so did Anna, which left just Gillian to receive Viv's attentions. Gillian is said to have laughed at the memory of being the only woman out of the three to continue to visit Viv.

While Viv was in jail she had given birth to young Viv and a number of people connected to Viv had called at the hospital to see the newborn baby. Dodgy Ray Hewitson, who was close to Viv at that time, took some photographs into prison, so that Viv could see his new son.

Although Gillian knew of the existence of Anna Connelly and Julie Rutherford, she continued to meet intimately with Viv. As for Anna, she thought that Viv was only calling to see the children. And both Anna and Julie did not know that Viv was still seeing Gillian.

Gillian asked Viv why he did not want to live with her and the children. Viv avoided answering her by telling her to wait until everything was finished. He used the excuse that she or the children could get hurt, but in reality he was living in Newcastle with Anna and her two children, so that argument goes out of the window, as there was more chance of something happening in Newcastle than in a little village with only one main road leading into it. It sounds like Viv was stringing Gillian along with his usual tactic of 'keep them hanging on and pregnant'.

When it was put to Julie that Viv begged to be taken back by Anna, she replied, 'I've heard it all before. I've heard the same lines when I was pregnant and Viv liked getting you pregnant, but he didn't like having the responsibility of the pregnancy, certainly not. I threw him out actually when he went back to Anna.

'We had a fight, because my house was nearly burgled and it was because he was late, so of course I went off in a tantrum and we ended up falling out. He came back the next day and he got the alarm fitted and then obviously he went back over to Anna's and came back weeks later, but then I wasn't interested, but it was all right because I was safely pregnant and you were safe for nine months. Nobody is going to fancy you for nine months.'

Did Viv feel that after the pregnancy he could return to Julie? 'He came back, yeah,' said Julie. 'You are his possession! That's exactly what you are, until he says different. He didn't want to lose anybody: he didn't want to lose Anna and he didn't want to lose Gillian and he didn't want to lose me.'

Viv was reasonably honest with Gillian, but how honest was he with Julie? Her view was: 'He wouldn't have dared! He was obviously open with Gill, but not with me, no! Obviously I knew that he was living with Anna. He used to come and confess, but that was after I had Callum.

'He was Anna's, because she could have him as far as I was concerned, but it doesn't stop you loving him. And I loved him and I still love the man, but I hated him at the same time. I knew for a fact that he was living with Anna then, but it didn't stop him from coming here.'

So Viv had never made up his mind that he was going to live with Anna? To this suggestion, Julie responded, 'Not likely! He had every excuse in the book.'

It was explained that Anna had said that Viv had no time at all to be able to have these trysts with Julie or Gillian.

Julie said, 'If she could keep an eye on him then she's a better woman than I am.'

As far as Anna was concerned, Viv did not have time for such flings, as he was always on his mobile speaking to her. He would be back from wherever he was within a short time and he would bring Anna her cigarettes because he did not like her going to the shop for them.

Julie reacted to hearing this by saying, 'I wasn't allowed to go to the ice-cream van.'

Was Viv frightened that Julie would run off with another man?

'I don't know,' said Julie. 'I just know he knew I wouldn't do it. Viv was dead for some time before I considered going out again. He was definitely insecure within.

'There was one night I went out and he was here at eight o'clock in the morning! My female friend and I had been out and we were lying in bed laughing and carrying on when he opened the door. He was just standing there because he knew I had been out the night before, which was when he was with Anna. Anna was, like, saying, "He's my sole property." Anna is silly,

'There was a mutual friend of ours, and he used to phone every day even when Viv and I weren't speaking. He phoned her every single day. It came to the stage where I stopped going to her house until after he died because she told him everything: what I had on, where I was going and everything.'

Viv's affair with Julie resulted in two children. There was talk of DNA testing and even of getting solicitors involved. Gillian gave the history behind the name of Jodie Annie, Viv's daughter to Julie: it was Viv's grandmother's.

Since this wrangle over DNA tests, it has been accepted that
Viv is the father of Julie's two children.

Queen of the Castle seems to be what Viv made all the women
in his life and, if the worst came to the worst, he shut them in
the tower, so to speak. By getting them pregnant, he made
them less attractive to other men and in this way he felt safe
to devote his time to the others.

Gillian felt on cloud nine to know all Viv's intimate secrets,
secrets that neither of the other two women knew, and clearly
the fact that their relationship was clandestine made him all
the more attractive to her.

She asked Viv not to lie to her, but his favourite saying to
her – one that both the other women fell for too – was that
he felt relaxed in her company and that her home was like a
sanctuary. That sanctuary, though, would last only a short
while, for Viv's watch was his master and time made him
hurry to his next appointment. "I've got to fly now, bye," he
would say.

Gillian accepted that she was one of Viv's 'harem' and she
went along with all he demanded of her. She said that Viv
used to hurry off faster to the bookies than anywhere else,
but he always rang her and he was never off the phone,
calling at all times of the day and night. Was he checking on
her whereabouts?

If she went out, she would return to find Viv had left
messages on the answerphone demanding to know where she
had been and why she had not come back home by 11 o'clock.
He would be at Anna's or Julie's place and she knew that to
call him there would have caused problems. Gillian had

somehow turned from being Viv's childhood sweetheart – he had 'acquired' her by winning a £5 bet with a fellow pupil that he would kiss her – to being one of the three main women in his life.

But Gillian was determined not to lose her relationship with Viv, even though it would have been easy for her to let him go and make of her life what she could. She wanted him regardless of a lifestyle which meant she was not his one and only.

It was suggested that Viv had made no financial arrangements for Julie's children when he died. Was Julie and Viv's relationship over after she had Callum? 'Well, it was over for that time, but it was on and off all the time,' she said. 'That would be it for a couple of weeks, then he came back in about the March and I was getting ready to go out and I didn't really see him much after that, but I used to keep in contact with him and he would call occasionally.

'He had paid for me to go on holiday, Primrose Valley, the four of us [Julie and her three children] in a caravan. I have an older son and two little ones and I went off with my cousin and I never heard from him until the Christmas. Viv had sent the money for us in 1993.

'He phoned me from hospital [where he had an abscess lanced]. I had never been on holiday with the little ones. He asked where I was going.

'"Yeah, that's OK," he said.

'So he sent me some money over via taxi. When I came back that was it. I never rang him. If he wanted me then he knew where I was.

Top: In happier times Viv Graham (right) and Denny Haig (left) socialise with Harry Thompson (centre) in their local pub. Harry was also tragically lost to violence.

Bottom: Viv put in countless hours of training to make himself so hard and fit.

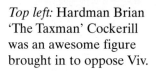

Top left: Hardman Brian 'The Taxman' Cockerill was an awesome figure brought in to oppose Viv.

Off-duty, Viv was a loving fiancé (*top right*), cheerful neighbour (*bottom left*) and keen amateur falconer (*bottom right*).

Top: Wheelers nightclub on the Gateshead side of the Tyne Bridge was where Viv had his first doorman job.

Bottom: John Henry Sayers is considered to be one of the most poised and unruffled of underworld figures ever to come out of Newcastle.

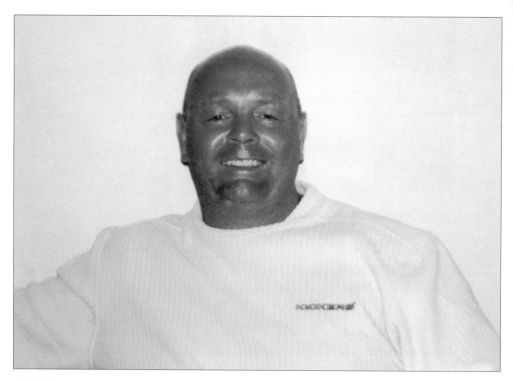

Top: Viv beat up club doorman Stuart Watson. CCTV TV cameras caught the incident and Viv was sent to jail for the attack.

Bottom: Viv was drinking in the Queen's Head pub (far right) moments before he was murdered.

Lee Duffy was proud to be known as Viv Graham's arch enemy.

Top: Lee (centre) with Lee Harrison (right) and a friend drinking at the Hacienda nightclub.

Bottom: Lee relaxing in the pub.

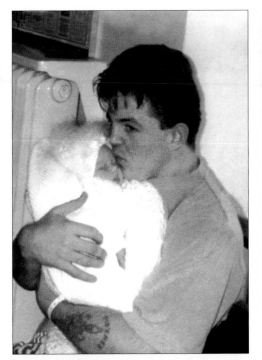

Top left: Lee holding the newborn Kattieleigh days after he was hospitalised for being shot in the knee.

Top right: Lee with Lisa Stockwell taking a well-earned rest in a jacuzzi.

Bottom: Lee and Lisa share a tender moment in the garden of the home they shared in Eston, Middlesbrough.

IN THE MEMORY
OF
VIV GRAHAM
LOVED AND RESPECTED
BY THE PEOPLE
OF WALLSEND

In Ever Loving Memory Of
LEE PAUL DUFFY
DIED 25th AUGUST 1991
AGED 26
A CHERISHED SON, A BELOVED
BROTHER, UNCLE AND DADDY
AND A BELOVED BOYFRIEND.

The North East's most feared men were
due to meet in a bloody showdown,
but the rivalry was cut short when they
each met horrifically violent ends.

Above and right: The gravestones of each
man.

Top: Viv's reputation as a hardman with a
heart of gold lead well-wishers to donate
a plaque in his memory.

'Then he sent Robbie Warton at Christmas. He was gone in December. I had not been seen going out with him in the last two years of his life as he had said, "It's too dangerous. You wouldn't believe the lifestyle I've got now, Julie."

'He came here and it seemed he had the world on his shoulders. He knew it was his sanctuary and he knew he was safe.'

Viv told Gillian the same thing – that he feared for her safety – yet he was living with Anna almost in the heart of Newcastle! If he felt threatened, what made him stay where he would have felt all the more vulnerable because his fiancée and her two children could have been hurt? He had warned Gillian and Julie of the dangers that he now faced, so it did not make sense that he should want to carry on living in a place where harm could come to those he loved.

Conjecture about this matter throws up a few possibilities. One is that he used this argument about safety to keep Julie and Gillian hanging on a thread for whenever he wanted them. In this way he could have his cake and eat it.

Julie quoted directly from one of the many letters Viv wrote to her while he was serving his three-year sentence:

'He said the only way he would get out of it was if he was shot. But it might just have been an excuse, as the man was full of excuses. The last two years of his life were totally different to the time we spent together, totally different.

'The exact words Viv wrote down are: "The job I do, you don't know when the fuck you could be killed … Julie, from what you've heard today you will see I live a dangerous life the only way I can get beat is by getting shot."

'That was letter number 134, written on 11 June 1990. This

is what he wrote when he was in prison, but his life was different when he left prison. The last two years. I don't know what happened.

'Yes, I know people used him. They always did, though; he was too nice. Viv's father said they used Viv as a moneybox, and that's exactly what they have done.'

Did any of Viv's supposed friends ever give Julie any support? 'Oh yes, they've asked, "How are you?"'

'"Fine."'

'I made a lot of enemies when Viv was in prison; they used to think things. This friend of Viv's has a lot to answer for as far as I'm concerned. He used to say to Viv, "She's working herself again!"'

'I used to get letters from Viv and he would write, "I don't want anybody but you to come in." That included his friends. He would also write, "I love my friends, but I'll see them when I get out."'

'That is the way Viv was, his friend would say, "It's her!" And so I was the villain of the piece.'

Was this man's friendship with Viv under threat?

'Definitely,' Julie said. 'I was the scarlet woman by the sounds of it. I think he did the same to Viv's dad. Viv had said that I couldn't put right the damage caused where his dad was concerned.

'I would say, "What are you talking about?" I don't know what he said. I hadn't ever spoken with Viv's dad. I was a threat to this man. He wanted to be the closest to Viv.'

So somehow this man and Viv had a falling out?

'Well, exactly,' Julie confirmed. 'I had said that to Viv's dad at the funeral. I said, "Wouldn't you have thought that after what he had done to you that you would realise the things he had said about me were lies?"

'He would say, "I know, I know."'

'My one and only concern is my son and what people have said about him. Viv just wasn't the same guy. He used to always be happy-go-lucky and couldn't give a monkey's. He didn't and wouldn't involve me in his private life. I didn't open the door to the press. I was just put down as Viv's secret love and I just let them get on with it. They had my name down as "Coffell" in the papers. I let them get on with it. I couldn't care less what they said. I wasn't reacting, so I thought, Dead end. Anna had made me react to this because of what she had said about my children.'

Anna reported that Alan Rooney, who at that time lived near Julie, took presents from her to Julie's children.

To this, Julie said, 'He brought the little one's car, a "Noddy" car, and he fixed it up. It was his birthday or something; Robbie Warton brought a big tractor and a couple of buggies. It was when Viv was banned from driving. Viv would phone and say he was sending them over; they never came when he didn't tell them to. Viv did not like me to have money; he thought if I had money I would go out. If we weren't speaking, then he would not give me money.

'When I first met Viv, it was in Finnigan's bar, at Felling, in Gateshead. Viv actually nipped my derriere; he wasn't as suave as people would believe. He wore a pair of Crimplene trousers and a flyaway-collar shirt, but he had the charm and he had the smile. Apart from that fact, he had a lovely bum. He nipped mine, so I had a little bit more to drink and then I nipped his.

'Apparently, he was with his girlfriend, Gill, and she had seen it and it had caused an argument, that's what I remember from it, and from then on that was it. We were an item for years and years as far as I was concerned, until he was murdered.'

To return to Anna, she commented, 'If he said, "Can I go out with the lads?" I would say, "All right, but can I go out with my sisters?"

'He would say, "No!"

'I would say, "Well, you're not going then."

'He was over the moon and would then say to them, "She'll not let me go out."

'He wouldn't let me go, so I wouldn't let him go. His friends would twist their faces. People used to say, "Wherever you see Viv, you see Anna. He never leaves Anna, the two of them are constantly together."

'I used to think it was that because maybe he had been sly with me by going with them [Gillian, Julie and others] and telling me lies. When he came out of prison he knew that I had never been with anyone. So I thought, Maybe he thinks I'm going to do back to him what he did to me and this is his insecurity with me.

'He said to me, when I gave him the ring back on the prison visit, "You'll love somebody else."

'I said, "That's one thing I'm not going to do, go with somebody just to pay you back for what you've done to me. That's just not my style."

'I wouldn't do that, get a man and think, Well, he'll be sick for what he's done to me. So he knew I wouldn't do that. I think he had this insecurity where he thought I would like to do back to him what he did to me. That's what I thought, anyway.'

11

THE GRASSHOPPER AND THE SQUIRREL

Eric and Hazel Graham are the parents of Viv. Eric prefers to be called Jack and from now on that is how he will be referred to. Asking to interview the parents of Viv was not an easy thing to do. Journalists had pursued them in the midst of their grief, at all hours. And there had been a big bust-up between Jack and a Denny Haig, a former colleague of Viv's, as a direct result of an episode of TV's *The Cook Report* that dealt with protection rackets and showed Viv in a poor light. And I was, after all, only another of those investigative journalists requesting a comment.

It might sound like this chapter is going to be about Viv, but it is not. It is dedicated to the two people who brought their little baby into this world with all the hopes that parents have for their children. Everyone's little Johnny is going to play football for England, make millions or become a great painter.

Viv's parents got to see their little Viv become big Viv. His achievements made them proud – the boxing medals and cups he won and the footballing skills he developed as a schoolboy – but they felt blessed, too, that he had a kind and gentle nature. If any parent can bring their child up to be like this, they have achieved far more than cultivating a winner of medals or prizes.

Jack and Hazel Graham were able to instil into Viv something that not many people could learn in two lifetimes: manners. Their honest, decent way of bringing up Viv and their other children shows that the old moral qualities have not completely died out.

Surrounded by fields, Rowlands Gill, where Viv grew up, looks like many a country area of England. There is one difference here, though, and that is that there is no snotty atmosphere of curtain-twitching. This is a down-to-earth, rural council estate where just about everyone knows everyone.

At first, my meeting with the Graham family was strained. Karen, Viv's sister, and her husband, Martin, were present in the living room, but one person was conspicuous by his absence: Viv's father. Jack Graham had not spoken with anyone about his son's death and, sure as hell, he did not want to talk to another interested party.

As I was talking to Mrs Graham, I could hear a creaking of the floorboards coming from an upstairs room. I was aware of the sound for a few minutes and I could tell someone was walking around, or rather pacing. Then I heard the stairs creak; someone was coming down. Everyone stopped talking and all eyes were fixed on the living-room door.

The silence created an air of expectancy and it was as if everything was happening in slow motion.

Slowly, the door opened into the dimly lit room and all I could see was a huge form looming towards me that seemed to fill the whole frame.

It was the eyes that I first noticed, dark and powerful; a nod and a wink and you shifted out of the way, sort of thing. The light just caught the shaven head of the tall and powerfully built Mr Graham; at least I hoped it was Mr Graham. Silhouetted as he was, he seemed larger than life.

What was I to do? I stood up and walked across the room with my hand out to clasp his. The worst that would happen was that he would chew it off.

'How do you do, Mr Graham, sir. Pleased to meet you,' I said in my best submissive voice. The hand that met my own size 11 seemed to engulf it; it seemed to be twice as big.

With that, the ice was broken and the best interviewee I have ever met took centre stage. This man should have run for Parliament, for Jack is a natural orator. He is a man's man and, although he has seen better years, he still has an aura of immense physical power. Even though he has suffered illness, he is still a man to be reckoned with by virtue of his worldly wisdom.

Before long, Jack was prompted into talking about the incident at Hobo's nightclub that led to Viv being convicted of a vicious unprovoked assault. 'Our Viv was at the court case,' he said. 'There was Michael Sayers, Davie Lancaster, Fish Tams, and there was a sixth lad and they were looking for him. He was going into Durham jail every week visiting them. I don't know if somebody must have tumbled, but it was weeks after because they chased him, busies [police] in their cars, and they caught him outside Durham.

'The busies had got the lot and fetched it in as an affray. If you'd seen the tape, from them going through the door to them coming out, it was only minutes. Three minutes; it took three minutes. Now then, there were two busies in Hobo's and they were on surveillance for drugs. They were from Tadcaster, they were Yorkshire busies; they weren't from here.

'The policeman said he had never seen a fight like it in his ten years on the police force. He said that our Viv started on Stuey Watson, moved off, two attacked him, kicking and punching, they came off and the other three went in kicking and punching.

'So that's six blokes kicking and punching one man and, if you look at the video, Stuey Watson comes out and he's hardly got a mark on him. How can they tell me ...? I mean, six old pensioners should have put him in hospital. You've got six blokes kicking hell out of him. They said to the busy, "Why didn't you show your warrant card?"

'They said, "We were on surveillance."

'They were asked, "What would happen if a lass was getting raped, would you have just sat back and watched it, like?" Viv got three years for it in the end.

'The thing is, there's been that much written in the press and said about Viv Graham, whatever happens to whoever or a friend of Viv Graham, it's in the papers.

'To signify how they got it wrong about him being a £2-million drug baron, I had to pay his car off. Me, like a silly bugger, had to go and put my name down.'

Jack said this to question how it could be, if Viv was making so much money from his alleged drug empire, he had to act as a guarantor for his son's car and subsequently take over the payments for it.

Hazel interjected, 'The bailiffs came here twice to take furniture out for this car money that was owed. The bailiff said, "There isn't sufficient in here to cover it, so I'll just tell them you haven't got anything." He was brilliant.'

In a way, Hazel was right, what could the bailiff have taken to cover the money that was still outstanding on Viv's Ford Sierra Cosworth? After all, this was a humble home, clean and comfortable, with all the items needed to make life bearable, but there was nothing there that could repay such a debt. Any bailiff taking items away from Jack and Hazel's home would have to have a heart of stone.

What about Viv's friends: could they have helped out? Jack answered, with a certain amount of anger in his voice that summed up his feelings about those who were supposedly his son's friends, 'I'll tell you, and you can put this in the bloody book as well: they weren't friends, they were hangers-on; he was a moneybox for them.'

Jack continued in the same vein, saying, with sadness in his voice, 'And he was a minder for them! That's what he was.'

He was speaking for a lot of people when he added, 'When they were with Viv Graham they were ten foot tall! "Oh, I know Viv Graham, good friend of mine," so people would back off.'

Jack related an incident in which his son exercised his right as a private citizen to carry out some late-night security work. 'At the top end of the village, a lot of old people live and they were forever getting robbed. So he went up and sat in an old woman's house all night, sat in the chair all night, waiting, and nothing turned up.

'So he went to a certain party and said, "Look, if another one of those houses gets done, I'm coming for you. Even if you haven't done it, I'm coming for you. I'm going to make a job of you, so spread the word, you're the one that's going to get it." It stopped.

'Christmas, before he died, when he was shopping with Anna, an old lady wanted a turkey. He said to Anna, "Keep her occupied." He went into a butcher's shop and came back and said, "There you are, mother, there's your Christmas dinner." They don't know about them things and when he sponsored the footballers and the boxing, things like that.

'He gave a kid [his friend Pip Wright] £500 the week before Christmas, he hadn't a penny, he couldn't get the kids anything for Christmas. Viv said, "There's no kid should get up on Christmas morning without presents, give me it back when you've got it." That's the way Viv was.'

Then Hazel said, 'He saved Rob Bell's life.'

Jack took up the story: 'If Rob knew that we were here, he would …' but, just as quickly as he had started, he moved on to another: "Wor Viv bumped into him [Peter Donnelly] in the Fish Bar in the Green Market [in Newcastle]. He was crying to wor Viv, saying, "Divent hit me." Viv said, "I'm not going to hit you, don't worry."

'You see, the trouble is …' Jack took a breath before going on, as if it was releasing a great burden to be able to say this to someone, perhaps for the first time, '… he couldn't be a bloody gangster at all, he was too soft. You get these that lend you money and, if you don't pay it, it's doubled and then you get a good thumping and then a leg broken the next time. He was too soft.

'Mind, when he kicked off, if he had a fight, he could go, there's nobody ever done it yet ...'

Jack reminded himself of his son's absence by saying, 'Well, they'll never do it now. He was hard, that way it was good, but, the other way, he was as soft as claggy taffy [sticky toffee]. He was as easy for a hard-luck story.'

'He could cry like any other man,' said Hazel.

'He was as soft as clarts that way,' added Jack.

Jack talked about the police. They tried all ways to get our Viv. When Viv came out of prison, they were following him in the car and taking photographs of him. They went around the town [Newcastle] and followed him all over and he just used to go, "All right, lads."

'But the surprising thing is, what a hell of a lot got on with him. From what I've heard, all the jumpy jacks are back in the town on the happy baccy and the stuff now, and people won't go back into the town. People are just petrified, where at one time you could go and sit and have a good night out with nothing to worry about.'

Then Hazel gave her account of meeting one of the Sayers family. 'I met Stephen Sayers when our young Viv [Viv's son] was poorly in hospital. He was a gentleman. I couldn't get over him; he was at the hospital at eight o'clock in the morning when I walked into the [Tyneside] General [Hospital]. He said, "I'm sorry I've met you under these circumstances." Viv was still in prison.'

Jack clarified how Stephen Sayers was out of prison before

his son. 'They got two years and our Viv got three. So they were out, and he was at the hospital to see the bairn. They were all friends then.'

Karen then threw in something that said it more succinctly. 'They were using him as a minder.'

After serving his sentence, Viv went his own way. Jack explained, 'Wor Viv was always a loner, though. I mean, if somebody said, "I'll fettle Viv Graham!" he would jump in the car and he would go to that place where this bloke had said what he was going to do. "Where's so and so? I'm here."

'They'd say, "He's not in."

'Viv would say, "Well, I'll be back tomorrow night."

'Where they take teams now! He didn't need that sort of backup. He would go in and he'd never been to that place in his life and wouldn't know the bloke from Adam. He had no fear.'

Viv got on with people. Manny Burgo was mentioned as an example, and Jack said, 'They had a fight [boxing as amateurs] and Viv brayed bloody hell out of him, because his old man said to Viv, "You did that to my son."

'Viv never boxed for years and he was finished with the boxing, but he still had the fight with Manny. Viv had not fought for years, he won the Northern ABA Championships in 1977, and he had three fights in the one night down South Shields to win it. He then went to Denmark to fight. He was in Liverpool and he got a frozen shoulder and he got beat. He just concentrated on weight training and running, but you know what happens once you start hanging about with lasses: training's out the window.'

Mimicking a woman's voice, Jack said, 'You think more of

bloody football than you do of me,' and we all laughed. 'You know what they are like. So he just pursued weight training.'

Hazel said, 'He was never in trouble with the police as a teenager, never. He [Jack] used to say to Viv, "Burgle anybody or rob them and me and you are finished," you know.'

Jack confirmed this. 'I said, if you ever come in here and have been doing a house or drugs, that's me and you done.'

On the way Viv would seek advice from his father, Hazel said. 'He used to come here on a Sunday morning after he'd been to the nightclub. We used to always have loads of company and he used to say to everybody, "Right, I want to talk to my father, everybody out!" It didn't matter who was in.

'In fact, when this came out about Viv, I didn't even know anything existed. We can't say.'

Here Jack helped her out. 'We didn't know half what went on, that was his business. He was a man for himself. You make your bed, you can lie in it. What you do is your business but, as I say, drugging and anything dodgy like that, I don't agree with, I've never agreed with it. As I say, he's a man for himself and we don't know half nor quarter of what he did or didn't do down there [Newcastle].'

Karen backed her father up. 'I always thought he had two separate lives because Martin and me started socialising with Anna and him. We started going to the town and nightclubbing. We used to get the feeling he didn't want us down there.'

Martin took up what Viv's sister said. 'Obviously, anything could kick off at any time where he was, so obviously it was for our safety as well.'

Jack spoke with wisdom when he added, 'It's a different ball game doon the toon. They can buy you at one end of the street and sell you at the other end.'

What about when Viv wanted to relax?

'We used to go shooting at Haydon Bridge,' Jack said. 'Everything just seemed to lift off him. I don't know how you explain it, but it was like waking up on a Sunday morning.'

'He delivered a ferret,' Hazel recalled. 'He sent it by taxi with a note: "I love you, Dad. Here's a present for you." It was a live ferret! The poor man [the taxi driver].'

Jack told how Viv came to send the ferret to him: 'There were some kids knocking a ferret around the street and wor Viv gave them £2. He said, "Here's £2, I'll buy that ferret off you." He then said to the taxi driver, "Here, take that, here's the address, give that to my father." The brother-in-law's still got it yet. He sent it all the way from Wallsend.'

Jack confirmed Viv's love of animals. 'He always had hens, we had his two dogs here: his Alsatian, Max, and the Labrador.

'When he got Buster he also got the Alsatian. He said, "I'll give the Alsatian to my father; I've still got the two down the garden." There were lads with pigeon lofts out the back and when he was young he used to get squealers, little 'uns, off the lads. He had about a dozen or more. We used to put them in a cardboard box and put them in the wagon and get away, over to Whitehaven and I would let them out.'

Jack then talked of how he has an aversion to reporters. 'That fettled me with television and reporters when he did that on the Thursday night and on the Sunday morning I saw the headline "£2m Drug Baron". I said they are not worth a bottle of pop. And then *The Cook Report*: they tried to make wor Viv out as bad as them that done that manageress up in

Manchester. I said it wouldn't have been as bad if that's what it was about, but it had nowt to do with security, protection, drugs, drinking.'

Jack expressed his anger, saying, 'If I had been a stranger and I had seen that on television I would say, "He must be a wicked pig, him!" People that didn't know Viv would say he was nasty, but it had nothing to do with the programme, but the buggers stuck it in about protection.

'So when I saw *The Cook Report* and I knew that things were wrong within it, I then wondered how many more *Cook Reports* are wrong.

'If I was walking along the Quayside and a little bairn fell in the Tyne and I dived in and got it out, there would be a little bit about that. But, if I walked down the Quayside and picked a kid up and hoyed him in the river, there would be headlines this big,' said Jack, holding his hands wide apart. 'I mean, murder, rape and anything like that, they make as gruesome as possible.'

Asked about Viv's apprenticeship as a doorman, Jack said, 'He was as green as grass when he started at the Hedgefield.'

Hazel disputed this, saying, 'It was in Burnopfield, the Travellers Rest.'

Jack continued, 'He started working in a number of pubs, as the person owned three, and he went through to Whitemare Pool [on South Tyneside] and he ended up at Finnigan's bar in Gateshead. That was where Viv had the fight with Paul Ashton. The fight went on up the road for about 20 minutes.

'They reckon Billy Robinson, Viv's mentor, stepped back to see what Viv could perform like. Viv played with Ashy for 20 minutes around the car park and Ashy was shouting and bawling at him to stand still so he could hit him. Viv was just bop-bopping; he was like greased lightning.

'Then he went to work at Wheelers, on the Gateshead side of the Tyne Bridge, just before you go over on the left-hand side; it's closed down now.

'He was with Billy Robinson then. The problem was, Viv was from the sticks and the townies didn't like this. They would say, "Where's he from? *What!*" A lot of them had the idea that no one was going to come in from the sticks and do anything to them, sort of thing.'

Jack was asked where the turning point came in the transition from Viv from the sticks to Viv of the town? Martin interjected to offer his view: 'As things progressed, he just became more popular.'

Then Jack said, 'More and more tried to down him. He won, and he won and he got his name more known and more known in the pubs and the nightclubs. The more that had a go at him, the more he beat. His name just spread like that, you know.'

Hazel began to talk about when Viv, as a boy, had run-ins with his peers. 'I used to fight his battles, Viv wouldn't fight.'

Jack offered a story about Viv's childhood. 'He fought out there with young Stubsy and Stubsy was knocking hell out of him. I said, "I'll bloody murder you, lad, for letting him do that to you. Give him some back!"

'I used to take him to boxing and he took to it like a duck to water. He had four things going for him that very few fighters have got – I mean street-fighting. He had speed, he had the wind, the stamina and he had the hitting power.

'Put them on that street or a football field and phew! They

just couldn't put it together, they don't know how to use their hands, and they depend on just strength and weight. You can be as strong as a bull but, if you're not fit, once you start puffing and panting you're finished.

'You're fighting some bugger and you start puffing and panting and he's still going strong! It's time for you to reverse, because you're going to get a tousing. Viv knew how to hit and the weight training gave him the strength. He put four down in less than four seconds. Four blokes in the bar.

'Anna's dad came up to Viv and said, "I was just going to give you a hand there, Viv." Bump, bump, bump, bump! Four left hookers and they didn't get up! Mind you, I'm not just saying that because he was my lad.'

What were Viv's fears?

To this, Hazel said, 'You know something: he was the most scared person of the dark. He was petrified, petrified.'

Jack said, with laughter in his voice, 'He would come in through the night, to go out the room he would open that door, put that light on and there's a switch to the top of the landing, he would put that light on. He would fly up the stairs and get hold of his bedroom door and hoy it wide open. Then he'd knock the switch on and go in.

'One night I said, "Oh, Viv, feed them dogs, son."

'Viv replied, "Aye, right you are, Father."

'He would go out the back, and I would sneak out of the front door and sneak down the garden, it was pitch black! He would shout at the dogs, "*Howway!*"

'I would go, "Urghhh!" The tins and the food would go up a height, and he's back in here like a shot.'

We all burst into spontaneous laughter at the thought of

this, and luckily we were all on the same wavelength to be able to enjoy a moment of nostalgia.

Jack talked of when he and Viv went shooting and how good a shot his son was. I know what you will be thinking, but don't. Viv was from the countryside and their way of life is different. A double-barrelled shotgun does not hold the same fear for these people as it would for a city dweller looking down the barrels of a sawn-off.

Similarly, game pie and salmon are things that people take for granted in rural areas. Shooting, hunting and fishing are their way of life.

Hazel looked across to Viv's sister and said, 'She saw him a few days before he died. She said to Viv, "What's wrong with your face today?" Viv said, "Oh, I'm just fed up, Karen; I'm on my way home, I'm sick of paying bills." Viv had just bought a house at the time.'

Viv's school days came up, and Jack said, 'I think he was a bit thicker than me when he was at school, wasn't he?' Jack's tone of voice when he said this was not condescending or patronising. Nor was it said in a disparaging way; it was simply the truth.

'It was only in my last three years at school that I picked up,' Jack said, 'and I think Viv did the same. Viv was obsessed with strength. He started with a Bullworker and, when he was working, he would put six more bricks in a hod than anyone else and it just went on from there.'

'He always covered his body with a big shirt,' Martin put in. 'He didn't go around with his chest hanging out.'

Jack continued, 'He looked far bigger when he was stripped than he did with his shirt on. What I put it down to is these old cowboy films. The gunslinger. There's always somebody wants to take your reputation. Well, as he went on, his reputation just grew and grew and more blokes tried to take it off him. He wasn't like a bully.

'Viv would say to me, "I was sitting there having a quiet drink and another one kicked off." I would ask him if he won and Viv would reply, "Oh, aye! I've knacked him. You can't even go for a quiet drink, there's always somebody wanting to have a go at you, man."

'He used to go out with Anna and they [troublemakers] would say, "He's on his own, we'll get him while he's on his own." He just got the reputation as a fighter and you've always got somebody to tell you what they think of you.'

Viv's heroes?

'Just his dad,' Hazel said. 'He worshipped his dad, nobody else.'

At this Jack was overcome with embarrassment and said in a low tone, 'I never heard him.' What he meant by this is that Viv did not openly say soft, namby-pamby things. But the point was taken about who Viv looked up to.

Jack continued, 'He liked the film *Zulu*, he watched that over and over again. It's a cracking picture.'

'He loved home cooking, you know,' Hazel added, 'and he used to get me to do a spotted-dick pudding, put it in the cloth and dish and he used to say to me, "Now, Mother, how long does this take to cook?" And he used to take it back with him to Daisy Hill and cook it down there. Christmas cake. I think everybody in Daisy Hill had a Christmas cake off me. Scones, pork pies. I think I kept Daisy Hill on them. The minute they came out of the oven, he would pinch them.'

How did Martin get on with his brother-in-law? 'Viv did little pranks on me, like throwing buckets of water out of the window. It must have been when I threatened him,' he said jokingly.

Martin used to train at a place called 'The Hut', in Highfield, near Rowlands Gill. Jack explained, 'It's just a hut, there's no running water or nowt like that, just up the steps, a door in, benches and weights and all the local lads go in there and train. You would just come home and have a bath or a shower after a session in there. It's got a brick foundation with wood sides. When it first started off, it was the St John's Ambulance Brigade base.

'When they started the weight training, they asked if they could use the bottom end of the hut; the other end was all stretchers and that sort of thing. Then the St John's Ambulance just sort of seemed to die out, nobody went to it, and the lads took it over and paid the council a rate. It's been there for 20-odd years now.'

The Hut is indeed still there and is an unbelievable sight, the sort of place that those seeking the eye of the tiger would train in – if they were hungry enough for that sort of thing! It is full of menacing-looking weight-training machines and other apparatus for self-inflicted torture. The facilities are few and it is the sort of place you would expect to see SAS men scrambling to get out of!

What advice could the Grahams give to anyone considering pursuing making places safer for others, as Viv had tried to do? Jack said, 'Leave it alone, because now it's a gun in life, it's not like me and you going outside and that's the end of it. They'll stab you or shoot you or get a team up or baseball-bat you. There's nowt like that now; you cross somebody and there's a team out the next bloody day, looking for you or they cross you and you get a team out looking for them. I think a lad now had far better mind his own business, because he's not going to win no battles; there are too many druggies.

'This bloody druggie business, I mean they're out of their mind, they'll stab you in the night and, when they wake up in the morning, they wouldn't know they'd done it. You haven't got to be a big bloke; you can be six stone nowt. You can put a knife in somebody or shoot somebody just the same as somebody of 17 stone can do. You see, a lot of these bouncers just look at a man. I know of a man, he's married and got a baby, he says, "Jackie, it's bloody crackers, man. You don't know when you're going to get a knife in you." This is what I mean!'

What drives people on to become a doorman and a troubleshooter of other people's problems? Jack's opinion was: 'Well, the doormen, the majority of them, have got backup in a club and, when they leave a club, most people don't know where they come from. At the same time, it beats working for a living.

'If somebody said they were going to do something to wor Viv, he wouldn't get a team together; he would go and sort it out himself. He never went with teams all over the place.

'That's just the way he was, he had no fear of anybody, he never carried a weapon. He never had a gun, a baseball bat or a knife, he just had his fists. If anyone had pulled a gun out on Viv, he would have stood his ground and tried to talk.'

Asked about Viv consulting him over an offer of work that came from Tenerife, Jack answered, 'I told him to keep away from it. I said, "Just stay clear of it." Viv was wanted to do their fighting.

'Not only that, I says, "There's bloody guns and all sorts over there. It's not worth it. You stop home."

'I mean when you're 20-odd or 30, you never think you'll get to 60, you're afraid of nobody and you never think what's going to come off. I didn't want him to go and he never went.'

On Viv and Higgins Security, Jack said, 'Higgins Security, they were from Birmingham, they wanted Viv to go and see them. I told Viv to let them come to him.'

Of all those people that Viv helped and made money for, Jack said, 'They weren't friends, they were hangers-on, he was a moneybox for them and a minder for them. He got the money from the doors on different jobs and that's all he was. What I mean is, he looked after their jobs for them. That's the way I mean he was a moneybox because, if anybody wanted a lend of money, he would lend them it. Any trouble, and he would go and sort it out for them. That's all he was to them, a moneybox.'

Of Viv's true friends, Hazel said, 'Viv had two genuine friends, Robbie Warton and Rob Bell. They both keep in touch, they come up here every so often. They are genuine people.'

Talking to Jack, you get the impression that he is more worldly wise than most people are. How did he acquire this wisdom? I asked.

'I was as thick as a chip at school, me, lad,' Jack replied, then Hazel interjected, 'You did the doors, though, when you were younger. You did the local dances.'

Jack played this down, saying, 'It was just the local dances;

there were no nightclubs then! Chains out of the collar and that sort of thing!

'It was not as bad as now, you had broken bottles, chains and flick-knives, but this drug business set it all off. Then you were hoyed out of the pub at ten o'clock and you came out of the dances drunk. Now, you get some of them in a right state, drinking all day and night, and they are on this bloody stuff. It's a different ball game in the town.'

Hazel may well have pinpointed something that attracted Viv into his profession when she said, 'He did it for the money; there was no money here for him. He hated going out at the finish, though. He would sometimes just stay in.'

Jack defended Viv as regards people calling him a doorman or bouncer. 'He wouldn't stand at doors. It got to the point that, if he looked after a place, then he didn't need to be on the door. Those on the door would say, "Mind, Viv Graham looks after this place. Kick off somewhere else, like."

'Viv suffered migraine, which he got from his mother. She suffers terrible with it. He used to take Paracetamol like a child eats Smarties.'

Was stress a contributor to these headaches as well? In Hazel's opinion, 'Definitely, stress brought it all on. Eh, I mean at times it was terrible. When he got that abscess and they said he was filled with steroids, what a load of codswallop! There wasn't a bit of steroid in his body. They said that about the steroid thing around about the time of his funeral.'

Jack added, 'I said to Viv, "Why do you need that for? I'd rather be 15 stone or 14 stone or ten stone of muscle and bone rather than be 18 stone of bloody water. It's like carrying two stone of bloody tatties on your back. One minute they're 16 stone, then they're 19 stone.'

'There was a time he had no neck, his stomach hung over his trousers and you ribbed him something rotten,' said, Hazel, looking at Jack.

Jack took up the story. 'He stopped doing the running; he was just concentrating on the weight training. I used to say, "Bloody weight training, aren't you? You want to get on that field outside the house and get running again."

'He would say, "Aye, Father, I'm going to get some of this off."

'"Well, you want to, then," I told him. "You'll meet a young Viv Graham, mind."

'I used to say to him that there's always somebody that's going to be bigger and stronger than him or younger than him. "Bigger, stronger, better," I used to say. "It doesn't matter if you live to be 60, you cannot beat a 20- or a 30-year old."

'There's always somebody coming up. Even if you're never defeated, then there's a time in your life when there's a young 'un who is good enough and fit enough to beat you, because you're getting too old. So I said, "There's always somebody in the world that's better than you somewhere, it doesn't matter who you are. Just look at your boxing. The best in the world can get beat. If you keep on with it, then the older you get, there's a young 'un coming up and he beats you." It's a fact of life.'

When Jack talked about stories in the newspapers of bent vicars, we all broke into laughter. Everyone will recall seeing a story sometime about such things on the front of the tabloids.

Sticking with the topic of the media, Hazel said, 'We had

letters put through the door saying, "We wrote nice things about Viv, if you'd only talk to us," and things like that. I went to the graveyard and photographers were following me there! I used to go before eight o'clock in the morning to keep out of their road. I used to do all sorts to keep away from them.'

Jack added, 'I opened the door one day and they were there, the television that was. I had to go to the inquest and two of them were in the street and they took my photograph; it was too late to stop them.'

He returned to the ecclesiastical side of things, saying, 'If I had my way, I would sack every vicar, Catholic father, rabbi – every religion, sack them all. There's been more bloodshed and murder through bloody religion in this world than anything else.

'My second wish, I would fetch Guy Fawkes back and give him all the bloody gunpowder he wanted.

'My third wish would be that Britain would have a ruler with bottle that would stand up to the rest of Europe. We don't want to be told by them what we can and what we cannot eat, what we can do and what we cannot do. See what I mean.

'On top of that, all of those asylum seekers. As soon as the boat comes in, I would turn it around and say, "Back to where you belong." Some of them are parasites living off us.

'If there were no religion, there wouldn't be any Catholics and Protestants fighting in Northern Ireland.

'You wouldn't have Muslims and Sikhs fighting. Everybody would be one, everybody would be the same.' Returning later to the subject of religion, Jack said, 'When I went into that house [Anna's], I just had to get out. Seeing that picture on the wall of the little girl having her communion, that did it for me.'

With surprise in her voice, Hazel said to her husband, 'Do you know something? I've never heard you talk as much in months. I'm pleased Steve and his chaperone have come tonight. It's done you the world of good.'

What Hazel said made it clear to me that Jack had been withdrawn in the past over the tragic loss of his son. In fact, here was a man who is a natural communicator with a great fund of stories and wise advice.

We then talked about Terry Scott, an associate of Viv's, who was there just seconds after Viv was shot. Jack said, 'When it happened, Terry said, "I'm your son." I've never seen him from that day to this. He just started to move in Viv's circles in the latter part of Viv's life and wasn't a mate of Viv's for years and years and years.'

Hazel said, 'Viv could have a fight with someone and then shake hands; even with Stuey Watson, he made friends and he was invited to his birthday party, but he wasn't a party lad. He was dead old-fashioned.'

'On a Saturday night he would got to the Railway in Walker [in Newcastle],' Jack said. 'A quiet pub. He would have a nice drink.'

We talked of Michael Sayers and Jack said, 'He [Viv] did say he had some trouble with Michael Sayers.'

Hazel put in, 'But, no word of a lie, that Michael Sayers pulled into the yard one Christmas and gave us a Christmas card and £100 when Viv was in jail.'

Jack went on, 'Everybody's all friends but, if you fall out, you can fall out, can't you? So you're not friends any more.'

What about Viv enjoying the odd bet or two on the horses?

Jack answered, 'I said, "You're crackers, man, put it away, salt it away." I asked Viv if he'd heard the story about putting his money away for a rainy day. I said to Viv, "Have you ever heard about the grasshopper and the squirrel?"

'He said, "No, what's that, Father?"

'I said, "The squirrel gathers all the nuts and it hides them all over the place. The grasshopper just jumps about and enjoys itself.

'"The winter comes, the grasshopper has got nowt to eat, but the squirrel's got all its nuts to eat. You're not going to be 30 all your life; you're going to get to 40, 50 and 60. You can't keep this game up at that age."

'He would say, "Aye, man, Father, I'm not bothered about when I get to that age. I'm living now, man!"

'When Viv used to go the boxing matches with Rob Owen, it would be "red corner, blue corner? I'll have £25 on the red corner." He didn't know what that kid was like; he hadn't a clue what they were like. He was just laughing and couldn't care less about what happened tomorrow. Live for today and let tomorrow worry about itself.

'Well, ye bugger, he was 34, but he had a good life. He had a good last ten or so years. Well, see, when I think back as well, I worked all my life and an insurance bloke came around and he said, "Get a pension out for when you retire?" I said, "Get away, I could be dead next week, lad. What good's that to me?"

'We won the pools at work in a syndicate. They said, "Buy a new wagon, man."

'I said, "When I park this wagon up tonight, I forget about it until tomorrow morning and, if there's owt goes wrong with it, then he's got to fix it. I want none of that; I could be dead in five years' time."

'It's come and it's just went as the years went on, it was all spent, but, when I was older, it's like what I said to wor Viv. I mean, maybe if I had invested that money or joined a pension scheme I would have had a good pension. I said the same as Viv and he was just doing the same stroke.'

Hazel told me that as long as Viv's dad was around he would not have married anyone, as his relationship with his father was more important to him. I could see this, as it was his father he worshipped and loved; it was him that Viv confided in and asked for his opinion on certain matters. Viv did not leave it to chance by seeking anyone else's advice.

On the question of Viv's finances, since this interview took place there have been a number of settlements by insurance companies and there is no further argument as to who has a claim on his estate, as it has been settled by legal means.

As the interview was drawing to a close, I sat looking at a family that was recollecting all sorts of stories about Viv. The fear that was there when I arrived had long gone and the barriers had been broken down. I still see them all in my mind's eye and my memory is of a warm, friendly family.

12
GENTLEMEN PREFER GUNS

While out in Newcastle for a night out on the town on 22 August 1988, Viv Graham's close friend Robert Bell was involved in some trouble when a fight broke out in the city's Bigg Market area. About a dozen people were involved in a fracas that led to three arrests by police for drunkenness and public-order offences.

It has been alleged that one of the people involved in the trouble was Peter Donnelly, 24. He was charged and prosecuted for assault connected to an incident between Bell and one of Bell's friends and subsequently found not guilty. It was said that the police were called and broke the fight up.

The Prosecution claimed that Donnelly went home and changed his bloody clothes. Later, the Prosecution alleged that weapons were brought into play to even up the situation. Bell was a formidable opponent to anyone by virtue of his power and size.

In a meeting I had with Peter Donnelly some years ago,

which was not in connection with this book, he said in relation to a different incident that Viv had called at his trailer home and, for some reason or another, trouble started. Viv lost control and humiliated Peter by giving him a good hiding in front of his family at the Glassworks caravan site in Leamington, just outside Newcastle.

In retaliation for this attack, Peter further told me, he went with a gun and found Viv in a Newcastle restaurant; he pulled the trigger and the gun failed to go off. This story was related without any prompting. Throughout our meeting Peter acted with the gentlemanly conduct of a cavalry officer. He came across as genuinely helpful over what I wanted to talk to him about. There is no need to patronise people such as Peter Donnelly. I tell it like it is. Judging by his demeanour, it was obvious that he was not a person easily rattled by things that had happened or could happen to him.

Going back to the incident in the Bigg Market, the Prosecution alleged that he returned to the Bigg Market armed with a shotgun and a carving knife. Of course, he was acquitted of all the charges, and naturally has no wish to incriminate himself and so leave himself open to renewed charges or a civil action.

It is further alleged that Donnelly had an accomplice with him, who was never identified, when he returned to Santino's restaurant looking for Bell just after midnight. Bell was sitting at a table with Viv and others when violence flared up.

The accomplice stayed at the front of the restaurant, armed with a large knife, while, it was alleged, Donnelly walked in and went towards Bell. The patrons of Santino's thought it was about to be robbed by a pair of villains.

Bell later admitted that he was half expecting something to happen. Even so, it must have been a sobering experience to be confronted by a man pointing a 12-bore at his face from a range of only a few inches.

A size-11 fist moved faster than an eye could blink and took hold of the weapon, and Viv's powerful arm twisted it from the attacker's grasp like taking candy from a baby. To do this must have taken a split-second decision by Viv, whose rapid reactions as a boxer clearly came into play.

Viv detested the use of weapons in a fight, which was easy for him to profess, considering his pugilistic abilities. No doubt what caused him to grab the gun was his anger that such effrontery should take place in view of his fellow late-night diners.

As Viv proceeded to smash the gun against the nearby wall, all hell broke loose and the unknown man standing guard brandishing a knife came forward and held the knife to the stomach of Bell's younger brother, 21-year-old Ian. Someone brought a chair crashing down on to the knifeman's head and that put him out of action.

The Prosecution alleged that Bell and Donnelly somehow ended up in the back alley of Santino's. A fight ensued. Bell was, it seemed at the time, mortally wounded from being stabbed in the shoulder and heart.

The heart being a pump, when punctured it still pumps, and Bell's squeezed blood out through the puncture wound like a fountain of Italian red wine. By now, Viv was on hand a second time. Allegedly finding Donnelly there, Viv threw a punch that was to break Donnelly's jaw.

Seeing the blood gushing out of his friend's body, Viv was

so angry that he lost control and lifted up a beer keg and smashed it off Donnelly's body. He took off his top and used it to stem the flow of blood from Bell's wounds while they waited for an ambulance.

An interesting comparison can be made with the injury to an artery sustained by Lee Duffy when David Allison attacked him with a knife. Duffy's blood flow could not be stemmed even with the use of clothing, and the wound was fatal. Bell, however, survived a similar injury.

Without a shadow of doubt, if Viv had not been there, Bell would have been a dead man. Viv deserved to be congratulated twice for saving his friend's life. The first time was when he snatched the gun away from the attacker, and the second time when he stemmed the flow of blood from Bell's wound.

How ironic that, a number of years later, it would be Viv's turn to be fatally wounded in a backstreet. He too would be held in the arms of a fellow troubleshooter, in this case Terry Scott.

Viv did not receive a bravery award or a commendation for this heroic action, or indeed any other recognition. Had he been a police officer or even an ordinary citizen, he would have been nominated for a bravery award, festooned with medals and plastered all over the front page of the *Daily Bugle*.

But Viv was a known hard man, and such awards would only be seen to help bolster his reputation. It was accepted that it was all in a day's work for a man like him to be involved in this sort of incident. What would have been hailed as an act of heroism for other people was regarded as an everyday occurrence in the life of Viv Graham.

Just like any other man, however, Viv had feelings. Just because he was a powerful man and his exterior never cracked in public, it did not mean he was not an ordinary human capable of emotion. The ordeal must have been just as daunting for him as it would have been for anyone else. The crucial difference was that Viv could react quickly with his disciplined boxer's mind and resolve a dangerous situation fast.

Later Bell was to recollect that it was four men, and not two, that had entered Santino's with guns. His injuries put him in such a critical condition that at times it was touch and go whether he would pull through.

As a consequence of this near-fatal injury, Bell lost his building business. Viv made a statement to the police, obviously aware that this could be a murder case if Bell did not last the night.

Eventually Bell recovered enough to make a statement, as did his brother Ian. They named Peter Donnelly as the attacker. Donnelly was remanded to prison to await trial.

The charges that were put to Donnelly were: attempted murder, wounding with intent, possessing a firearm without a certificate, having a firearm with intent to endanger life and having a firearm in a public place. If found guilty, he could be sure that the keys to his cell would be thrown away for 15 to 20 years, if, that is, he did not receive life imprisonment.

Bell suffered from post-traumatic amnesia: he could not remember what had happened or recall who had attacked him. Ian Bell was unable to identify the man with the shotgun or the knifeman who attacked his brother.

Viv was giving evidence and was cross-examined in court but was unable to identify the two attackers. He said he had lied to the police about the identity of Peter Donnelly, whom he had named in a statement to them at the time of the incident, and that it was he himself who had inflicted the near-fatal knife attack on Bell.

The jury, unsurprisingly, acquitted Donnelly and found him not guilty of attempted murder. He was further cleared of the remaining charges and walked free from court.

Donnelly left the area and went to a travellers' site at Hull, where he stayed for some time. In time, Donnelly returned to Newcastle and became involved in a number of other criminal activities.

I want to finish this chapter by looking at a strange anomaly. John Henry Sayers, the brother of Stephen and Michael, was released from prison after serving a long sentence for robbery. He wanted to set up a taxi company because he had finished with crime and he knew if he so much as farted in the wrong direction the police would lift him. When John Henry, as he is known, made representation to Newcastle City Council for a licence to run a minicab company, the police attended; the council had a war cabinet and rejected it. By contrast, Peter Donnelly, a convicted fraudster, was able to run a security company and receive payment from North One and Newcastle City Council and to draw money from a publicly and EU-funded project.

Peter Donnelly appeared before Newcastle Crown Court in a sophisticated 'long firm' fraud case that involved a Welsh slate company being ripped off to the tune of £23,000. Donnelly had previous convictions for dishonesty, burglary, resisting arrest, Section 18 assault (resulting in 18 months' imprisonment), theft, road-traffic offences, drink-driving and fraud.

Glen Gatland, defending in the fraud case, told the court, 'Mr Donnelly is employing over 40 people, his VAT, Tax and National Insurance are being paid. In a VAT check, the VAT man came up with nothing in the company. He arranges contracts. The offence was committed 22 months ago and his business is very successful and Mr Donnelly makes an offer of full compensation to the slate company and to pay prosecution costs if given a suspended sentence.'

Mr Gatland even went so far as to suggest to Judge Crawford QC that the sentence on Donnelly be deferred for three months.

'People can't buy their way out of prison!' the judge said.

13
THE LAST TANGO

For the last 15 months of Lee Duffy's life right across the North-East, there was a lot of talk of the Duffer and Viv getting it on in a winner-takes-all fight. We all have secret fears masked by a thin veneer of bravery; fears that sometimes break free from their shackles for all to see. I feel that Viv may have harboured a secret fear of fighting Lee Duffy. It was a fear not of the clash itself, but of what would follow. For, even if Viv won the fight, he would still have lost his kingdom.

It has been claimed that, if the Sayers were to turn up with Lee Duffy in tow, Viv was going to be a little bit nicer to them than he would have been without the Teesside hard man at their side. It is said that a fight was organised between Duffy and Viv in the Havana club, in Middlesbrough, but Viv did not turn up. However, this has proven to be a rumour and nothing else.

Then there was talk of a second attempt to organise a fight between the two giants. Here the rumour was that Viv, thinking he was going to be shot, once again didn't turn up. Some say he remained at home emptying his bowels.

A figure from the Teesside underworld said, 'No doubt about it, Viv was a very hard man, but I don't think Viv would have beaten Lee. Viv was big and strong, but the Duffer had a psychopathic streak that Viv didn't have!

'Something the Sayers might have been worried about was that, if Lee and Viv had got their heads together, then they might have blitzed them clean out of the water.

'But, considering it was going to come off, Lee was permanently up the Mayfair nightclub [in Newcastle] all the time, constantly up Newcastle, but Viv wasn't down here.

'There were two arranged fights and Viv didn't turn up at either of them! Viv had a few doors up there and Lee went around and taxed a few of Viv's men. He wanted to put it on Viv's toes because he hadn't turned up.'

Adding to this story, Duffy's friend Lee Harrison, from Middlesbrough, claims, 'One Saturday night the Duffer went around the Bigg Market nightspot in Newcastle and knocked all the doormen out, first one pub, then the other one, then the other one and so on.

'I dropped Lee off while he went and done it and he was on his own. I've even dropped Lee off in Moss Side [in Manchester] on his own, when he chinned a doorman in a kitchen. Lee was wearing a white rainhat at that time.

'When he chinned them in the Bigg Market he said, "Go and tell Viv I'm here, get him here, go and tell your boss I'm here!" They all ran a mile, including Dodgy Ray [Hewitson].'

Tommy Harrison, Lee Harrison's father, says, 'People say Viv wouldn't go [to fight Duffy] because of the Sayers, but they were just young lads. When Lee [Duffy] went and knocked Graham's doormen out, where was Viv? If Viv believed he was going into a trap in an organised fight with Lee and then Lee goes to Newcastle and knocks his doormen out and tells them to go and tell Viv he was there, then he should have come, shouldn't he?

'I've worked all the doors, I've fought everybody you want to fight and, if a man had come and knocked my doormen out, then I'd have had to go and see him.

'That night he went looking for Viv: bang, bang, bang, and it cost them nothing. Viv called into my house, as he was passing, but how do you pass?

'Viv said to me, "I'm not frightened of nobody, me, you know. I'll fight anybody."

'I said to Viv, "So will Lee, but why? Who's going to benefit out of it, who's going to benefit out of you and him having it off? Why don't you two just graft together?"

'Viv Graham never came to the Havana club; it was just a rumour. A fight was going to be held in a warehouse outside Newcastle. He came to see me when it was all getting out of hand; it was like the old cowboy thing, wasn't it?

'I said, "Use your heads: you've got Newcastle in your hands and Lee's got all of Teesside in his hands. What the hell you want to be running around fighting with other people for, I don't know."

'But Lee had this thing about them [the Sayers]. They were going to look after him. I think that was the last tango: he didn't need them. He didn't need any money, he could go into a bar or a pub or a club or a restaurant, they'd invite him into the place.

'I'd say to Lee, "If you can wine, dine, eat, taxis for nothing, then what the hell do you want to be going up there for: ham and eggs?"'

Lee Harrison said, 'I flew to Jamaica and one of the people I bumped into said, "Where are you from?"

'I replied, "Middlesbrough."

'He asked, in a broad Jamaican accent, "You know Lee Duffy, man?"

'He knew straight away and he hadn't been brought up in England: he was a full Jamaican.

'He said, "I was in jail for a week and he came on to my landing and started throwing everyone over the top of the landing."

'At that time, Lee's name was bigger in the jail than it was outside.'

Others had an interest in Brian Cockerill's fighting power, and two in particular wanted to see a match between Cockerill and Viv Graham.

The Tax Man himself explained to me what happened: 'Stephen and Michael Sayers were willing to put £50,000 up for me to fight Viv and, if it had come off, then they'd have been able to say, "We've got a better fighter than you now." They thought they could manipulate us to their own ends!

'I was in a rave club and I was talking to Robbie Armstrong, who was Viv's partner, and I'd had a fight with a big lad from Stockton the week before. I'd knocked him out and Robbie said, "Do you know a lad called Cockerill?"

'Well, of course, Robbie only knew me as "Big Bri". He didn't know my second name was "Cockerill".

'Robbie went on to say that the kid I'd knocked out had offered Viv Graham £10,000 to come and fight this "Cockerill guy".

'Robbie said, "What do you think he'll do?"

'I said, "I think the big fella will beat him," and he went, "He's that good!"

'I laughed and said, "It's me, you daft cunt."

'He said, "You're joking," and he couldn't believe it.

'About a week later Robbie said, "Viv doesn't want anything to do with that fight, you know."

'I said, "What fight?"

'He replied, "Stephen and Michael put the £50,000 up."

'I didn't even know anything about it. What they were going to do was put a fight up in a warehouse in Gateshead or wherever it was, or Newcastle, and they were going to charge £10 a man to come in and watch it.

'They'd done all this behind my back without me even knowing. Robbie was saying, "The fight's supposed to be next month," and I hadn't a clue what was going on.

'Anyway, I goes to Newcastle to see Stephen and Michael. I goes in the nightclub and they'd only done it because they knew Viv Graham was coming in that night, but he never came in.

'I heard Viv did a lot of bad things with lads up in Newcastle; he invited Stevie Hammer [Eastman] out and then has a punch-up with him and punches him in the face. That, for me, was out of order, you know.

'When I was inside [prison] with Geordie kids, they used to say that he was a bastard for doing that. He'd get you up, get you pissed, put his arm around you and say, "Let's have our photograph taken," and then he'd punch them in the face. He was terrible for it.'

When the name Lee Duffy was mentioned to Viv's father, Jack, he spoke candidly about the man. 'Duffy said wor Viv wouldn't meet him, wouldn't have anything to do with him.'

Duffy came to Newcastle from his manor of Middlesbrough a few times looking for Viv so as to have a fight. As you've already heard, he beat some doormen up to try to flush Viv out of hiding. Such an act on someone else's territory was seen as a powerful insult, as if to say, 'I spit on your grave.' But Viv knew what was being plotted and did right to stay away. It's difficult to discover the truth here, but, assuming these doormen would allow Duffy to do that, other doormen would have come from the surrounding pubs to help out.

It has been claimed that the Duffer arrived in Newcastle in the back of a van and that as it was going through the city centre he threw open the rear double doors and shouted, 'I am the god of hellfire!' If this is true, it shows that the Duffer was not scared of Viv. It is further claimed that, when word got back to Viv, he decided to stay at home and switched his phone off.

The story goes that Viv felt awkward about meeting this man. But Viv's father feels strongly about this and offered his own explanation: 'Not likely. Duffy couldn't bray wor missus. What a load of bloody tripe.' It was explained to him that people wanted Duffy to settle their scores with Viv, but that this was only hearsay.

A fight was set up and it was arranged to take place in a warehouse in the Byker area of Newcastle. Viv's reason for not turning up was because he had been warned about certain people who would be there in the crowd watching. Even if he beat Duffy, he thought the set-up would result in him being murdered anyway.

He was a fine, strapping lad who had made a name for himself on Teesside and could handle himself as well as take a good punch. But Duffy was a pawn in a much bigger game than he could have known.

At one time Viv was an associate of the Sayers but, after he was sent to jail for beating up fellow doorman Stuart Watson, after finishing his sentence he went solo. Working as a troubleshooter for publicans, he now made sure his territory in the city's East End was off limits to just about everyone. Everyone. This closed down the possibility of drugs being sold on his patch.

Who could be brought in to sort out Viv Graham? No one in Newcastle was capable of the task, and even if there had been someone he would almost certainly not have wanted the unenviable position that Viv had chosen to hold in his campaign to drive out drugs.

Duffy was the hard man who was drafted in. He had been having a bit of a hard time in Middlesbrough, where it seemed that, no matter which way he turned, someone was out to get him. He was offered the opportunity to take over 'things' in Newcastle, but there was just one problem: he would first have to beat Viv in a winner-takes-all fight.

Just supposing that monumental fight had taken place and Duffy had beaten Viv, the tables would have eventually been turned on him by his hosts. How long would it have been before Duffy decided he was going to have it all for himself? He would have become ambitious and would have become a threat to those who had brought him in for their own gain. What goes around comes around.

Looking at the other scenario, where Viv beats Duffy, it would not have been as cut and dried as that because there was a faction dedicated to getting rid of Viv at any cost. As a result, he would have been killed at the proposed fight. He had turned lemon and people were starting to see him in a different light to that of being a pub and club troubleshooter. So, he would either have been killed while fighting Duffy by a knife or other attack on his back by the spectators, or shot dead at the end of the fight. And Viv knew this!

They would have been over Viv like gremlins, since access to the East End of Newcastle was needed at all costs, even at the cost of people's lives. Nothing mattered to these people. Viv had a family and friends, but in the end friends soon leave the fold, leaving relatives to grieve on their own.

Viv and the Duffer never did get to meet in battle. The two gladiators, with their huge reputations, were simply reduced to two little chess pieces in a much larger conflict: the drugs war.

14
WHEN YOU LOSE IT COMPLETELY

We've considered the damage that the Duffer could inflict with his bare hands. Now let's compare this power with the iron fist of Viv Graham.

Within the space of a few days, Viv had been a witness at an attempted murder trial and been shot at by a masked gunman, and now he was in court again to face a charge of GBH. This stemmed from an incident in February 1988 and here he was, in May the following year, standing in the dock wondering when it was all going to end. He faced a custodial sentence, but his guilty plea had cut some ice with Judge Angus Stroyan QC.

The judge heard how Carl Wattler was rushed to hospital for emergency surgery to remove a large blood clot at the base of his brain after he was found lying unconscious outside Baxter's pub in Newcastle. A scan had shown that an operation was needed at once, otherwise he would certainly have died.

FIGHT TO THE DEATH

Mr Wattler was subsequently left with nerve damage that caused blurred vision in one eye, headaches and a limp. After the operation he spent quite a bit of time in intensive care and had to be put on a ventilator to assist his breathing.

The assault occurred after Mr Wattler allegedly failed to finish his drink quickly enough when asked to at closing time. Viv, it was claimed, had acted a bit hastily, but admitted having punched Mr Wattler in the mouth.

What happened after that is somewhat unclear. It was said that there was a confrontation in the street when Viv went to lock the pub doors. Mr Wattler was apparently getting the better of Viv when a friend of Viv's, who was working the door with him, intervened and struck Mr Wattler across the head with an iron bar. This would account for the damage Mr Wattler sustained in the attack.

It is not the intention here either to glamorise Viv's life or to make him look worse than how the public viewed him.

No contact has been made with Carl Wattler to seek his side of the story, and my apologies to him if he reads this and finds it somewhat different to his account of the events. After all, it is he who was the victim of violence.

The sentence imposed on Viv was rather light and he could think himself lucky that he received an 18-month prison term, suspended for 18 months, and was ordered to pay £500 in compensation to his victim, which seems a rather paltry amount in relation to the damage caused.

It would mean that if, within the 18 months, Viv should become involved in any further trouble and be brought before the court again, he could have the remainder of that sentence added to any other sentence given by that court.

This, you would think, would be a deterrent to most people.

By all accounts, when Viv hit someone he would use a degree of force proportionate to their size. If they were knocked out he would, in some cases, catch them in mid-fall, before they hit the ground, to prevent them receiving further injury. Maybe that was after this incident of Mr Wattler receiving such horrendous injuries.

It was a close call for Viv. Imagine how different things would have been if, say, Mr Wattler's injury had been fatal because the blood clot had not been discovered by the hospital surgeon. Viv would have been banged up for a few years and might have still been alive today as a result of the different turn of events. It seems that when Mr Wattler's life was saved by emergency surgery it may have sealed Viv's fate. For Carl Wattler would have had to die for it to have had enough effect on Viv's life to make him change his ways and so avoid his eventual fate.

It is said that Viv always warned rowdy people three times to behave themselves. Maybe it was this incident that first caused him to do so.

I leave it to you to decide whether Carl Wattler was hit by an iron bar or only by Viv's fist.

15
THEY CALL HIM VIV

The man who holds the key to the riddle of Viv Graham's true nature is publican Peter Connelly, Anna's brother and Viv's prospective brother-in-law. Peter, not to be confused with Peter Donnelly, was like a relation and closer to Viv than any friend.

'He [Andy Webb, a former body-sculpture winner in the heavyweight division of Mr Great Britain, with interests in leisure facilities around Newcastle] came here and he was crying, and he asked if I would take him across to Viv's graveside. When we got there, he knelt there and sat there for an hour crying, showing his feelings.

'People would get in contact with me to ask Viv if he would come and look after their pubs. The breweries would say to the publicans, "Get in touch with Peter Connelly. He'll see his [prospective] brother-in-law. Maybe he can sort something out for you."

'We did it in a fair way. We didn't say, "Either you give us this" or "Pay us X amount of pounds and I'll look after your pub." All the publicans drank with me in this pub [where this interview took place] and, if they had a problem, they would come to me. If you had five or six characters in your bar and they want to make it into a loud bar, noisy bar and start effing and blinding and swearing, then other people aren't going to use your bar, so the trade was dropping off in some of the pubs.'

(It was common knowledge that even the police passed Viv's name on to those in need of his assistance and advice about security.)

Asked what would make these people come into a bar behaving in such a manner, Peter said, 'It would probably be their local bar, it would be close to where they lived. Lots of the pubs in Walker and Wallsend [areas of the East End of Newcastle] were all getting lots of trouble. A particular publican asked if I could bring Viv down. The troublemakers were pissing in glasses, urinating at the counter. They weren't great big, hard people.

'When Viv first came on the scene, they didn't realise his capabilities; they didn't realise how big and powerful he was until he got up to them. I saw it on one occasion when a guy said, "Peter, I've had enough of this."

'There was a particular family in the Walker area of Newcastle who weren't hard, but they were a bit crackers! They are a known family; I know them and get on with them, but Viv was working for the publican. I couldn't say, "Viv, don't give them warnings because I know them." He always gave them three warnings. You got a first warning, a second warning and then, after the third warning, you had to be clipped.

'This particular guy used to cause trouble in quite a nice pub in Walker called the Stack, and Viv went in and got hold of this man and within seconds – and this man was a big lad as well – the pee was running down his legs. Even though the manager was still a little bit frightened to say anything at the time, the next time the lad came in, the manager threw the lad a packet of Pampers, and everybody started laughing at this man who was supposed to be a tough guy; that was one.

'Then we would go on to another bar called the County. Viv would say [to the publican], "What can you afford?" He didn't say, "I want £100!" And the reply was, "Fifty pounds a week, Viv. I won't miss £50 a week. If I get rid of these two particular people, then this bar will pick up again."

'So Viv went behind the bar and started pulling pints in the bar and started serving people as if it was a family pub, his pub!

'It was, "A pint of Guinness, Viv."

'Viv was laughing away and carrying on.

'"A pint of lager, Viv."

'And these people stopped, literally point blank, and never went back in the bar again.

'The atmosphere was different in the pubs, the nightclubs and the social clubs. He didn't drink, you know. He only drank orange juice and occasionally a Guinness; if you ever bought him a Guinness, he would get really happy and enjoy himself. You could have a good laugh with him. It was great and everybody was happy.

'I got a phone call from a Bass publican; it was a pub off Norham Road, up in North Shields. This landlady had been petrol-bombed, she had a child on the premises; she couldn't take much more, but the breweries said they would pay to foot the bill. So, obviously, then we said, "Well, it's £500. It's a one-off thing and we aren't coming up every week."

'We got the address of these people who done this, knocked on their door and they were warned there and then! There was nobody got hit or anything like that and that was the end of the trouble for that publican up until Viv was shot, and then all hell broke loose! Obviously, everybody that ever got barred from pubs turned up. There was big parties, everybody went on a rampage, all those pubs got it that night.'

Even though Peter admits he has a criminal record for violence, for two assaults and GBH, he was granted a publican's licence. He says it seemed highly unlikely that he would ever get a licence under such circumstances.

'I was doing quite well and at that time I didn't hold a publican's licence or anything like that. The police asked to see me and I came down. They said, "Peter, it's come to our attention that you are trying to run a pub and we are thinking about letting you have your own licence." Which I thought was great, but because of my criminal record, it was unlikely I would be allowed ever to get a licence.

'It was 15 years since I was last convicted. I took the wrong route and mixed with drug dealers but, at the time, they were petty. They went in heavy-handed, that lot did; they burst into bars and smashed the place up and even took coffins to bars and did horrible and nasty things. I was with that clique for a short time because, at that time, I didn't have any money.'

Back in the 1960s and 1970s, a forerunner to Viv in the Newcastle underworld was Harry Perry. Known as 'H', Harry could use his fists, but he was said by some to have a short fuse and could blow for the slightest of reasons. Peter was asked about the man's connections, and said, 'Harry was there, it was one of Harry's operations in his time. He was the boss way back then; Harry and me had quite a close relationship then. We were sent in to do the business and they got the message, one way or another.

'The main nightclub where most underworld figures met used to be Billy Bottos. All the Newcastle big-name gangsters headed there in those days, [as well as] the Krays, and even Joe Louis.'

Peter knew some of the patrons of Billy Bottos and he remembers one in particular. 'One of the greatest men that I admired, more than anything, was a man called Jimmy Walker. I was at his funeral. His father had him fighting three fights a day for half a crown [12½ pence] a time, his knuckles were out here.'

Where did these fights take place? Peter was asked.

'These were the bare-knuckle days,' he replied. 'Under Pottery Bank, under the bridge, in different places, and the Quayside. He met Viv lots of times and Viv loved him.

'Viv would sit and listen to some of his stories. And he had the greatest stories in the world to tell. I've always wished that before he died someone would write a book about Jimmy Walker, because his stories were far greater than you could ever say about Viv. There were some belters. I would sit for hours and listen to them.

'They cut Jimmy's legs off three times, you know.' Peter indicated the places by pointing to his own leg and saying, 'There, there and there. He had fluid in his legs, until eventually his legs were off and it was just a body that they were carrying about. He lived through all of that, but died from pneumonia a year later.'

Was he a hero to Viv?

Peter said, 'He fought a Dutchman and at the bottom of the plate [winner's trophy] was inscribed: "The man who invented bottle", which was great because he was the man until Viv came along, and Viv obviously, to me, was the man who had all the right bottle in the world, and I've seen some awesome things when Viv was fighting!

'We once got called to a pub in North Shields in which we got paid £200. The man used to have a pub across here called the Queen's. When Viv very first came to Newcastle, that was the first pub he started to run in the East End of the city. A man called Denny Haig was working with Viv at that time.' (Denny Haig is from Highfield, near Rowlands Gill, where Viv grew up. Denny was featured in *The Cook Report* exposé mentioned in Chapter 11.)

Peter went on, 'I didn't hold any grievance against Denny until what he did to Jack [Graham], and then I was really annoyed. I know he's quite old, Denny, about 40-odd or 50, but Jack, to hit Jack! And Jack's never ever harmed anybody.

'They all seemed to jump on the bandwagon after Viv was gone; they all seemed to jump on his back and everybody was in his pockets! They'd only ever got money off Viv, he supplied their wages.

It may well have been that Denny Haig was misquoted in the TV documentary. This led to a confrontation between him and Viv's father.

Peter's ex-brother-in-law was David Lancaster, one of the

group that was involved in the assault on Stuart Watson in Hobo's nightclub. The whole affair is tangled.

Peter said, 'You could see by his [Watson's] face he knew what was going to kick off. Viv slung him about a bit, but Watson never went down; he blocked well and he covered well. You didn't see any photographs of Stuart Watson after it. You didn't see how bad he was.'

Peter described the fight, 'They went on about how heavy he [Viv] was and how he flung him [Watson] about like a rag doll, this, that and the other. I think it was just his [Watson's] jacket was too big for him, so it looked worse than what it was; it was never as awesome as that.

'There were four tapes, four cameras, actually on this fight. You were getting the back before the front; you were getting the wrong sequence. It came out the wrong sequence, not the way the event actually happened. It was nothing. I've seen a lot worse than that.'

Peter confirmed how people would use Viv's name for their own gains. 'Any nightclub where people went to, they'd say, "I'm Viv's pal," just so they would get in. They never ever knew him from Adam; they had never ever met the man.'

Viv was well known on Teesside and would travel down there each week, to nearby Spennymoor, where a weekly rave was held in the Venue. Peter confirmed that Viv made this weekly trip. 'He had to show his face to let them know he was in charge of it.'

Viv's generosity, at times, was overwhelming. On Christmas Day, a week before Viv was gunned down, he gave his friend Pip Wright £500. Wright was hard up for cash and Viv was generous that way.

Of Terry Scott, Viv's associate who held his head as Viv lay dying on the ground, Peter said, 'I've only seen Terry Scott once since he phoned me from the hospital and said that Viv was dead. I saw him once when I went into a nightclub in the town. It was a nice summer's night and he just sat outside the door with his arms folded and he just looked at me and I walked in. It was just that we didn't have anything to talk about.'

What about Rob Armstrong, who was one of Viv's closest friends until a few years before his death? What I am getting at here is that, if Viv had had a 'brother' who was just like him and they worked hand in hand like the Krays, or like the Richardsons, they would have defended each other if something had happened to one of them.

But, because Viv did not have this support system, there was no continuity to his defence. And, although the Connellys were as close as he was going to get to a family, it was not as though they were related by blood.

What about all those people and his friends? I asked Peter. 'They were just like rats leaving a sinking ship,' he told me. 'They were super-hard when he was there, but soon as he was gone they became nothing, they were just weaklings. He was their strength. What was going to happen to them as long as he was there? It was him that was always going to be in the front line; it was always going to be him that was going to be …' Peter talked fast at this point, half-finishing a sentence before moving on to the next: 'They knew his capabilities and knew nothing was going to happen to them, and it was just a free ride for them and there was as many as there could be that got on to the bandwagon.'

And what of the stress Viv endured? 'I think Viv took too much on; he was doing far too much. Later on, drugs became a big thing and they started coming in. They weren't there at first; they started moving very fast and there were quite a few drug dealers. I didn't realise there were so many drugs about and they all wanted to be in on the club scene. That's where they were sold. Es became popular, different types of Ecstasy tablets. Viv was never involved in any type of drug dealing.'

A story was related, on hearsay, to Peter about Viv being asked by a man in a Newcastle nightclub to sort out some trouble with the two heavies who had allegedly taken his Es and his money while he was in the toilets: 'He went crying to Viv saying that his drugs and money were taken from him. Viv went and knocked the two heavies out and gave the man his things back.'

Peter said about this, 'I don't know why he did that, but I heard about it. It was a stupid thing to do, but Viv was like that and he thought he was helping out. They weren't Viv's drugs. There was another girl in who was a big drug dealer, she had plenty of money. The Sayers got involved and beat her and her man up there and then in Madison's. Viv didn't intervene; he just kept out of it. He stood back and didn't get involved in it.

'A drug dealer asked Viv for a loan of £500. The man offered to pay Viv £600 back. I don't know if he loaned him the money, but that's the way people went on. Viv had no idea of other people's motives for wanting to borrow money.'

Peter must surely have seen a number of changes in Viv from the time he first met him up until his death. To this suggestion, he replied, 'He used to love going to the gym for half an hour or an hour; he would use Andy Webb's gym and they would end up having such a laugh.

'I never ever touched weights, but I was watching him as they put some weights on the bar. It was awesome, the weights they were putting on for him! Off he goes, he was bench-pressing it, and it was great to see him doing this and everybody would clap and cheer. Then they would put a bit more weight on and he would just press the weight that nobody could bench-press.

'Each time, he was getting bigger, you could see him getting bigger, but then he was getting little side-effects. He was complaining about certain things, he was aching and he didn't feel well at some stage. He had an abscess on his leg. [Viv at this time was taking steroids.]

'Bad-temperedness started creeping into it. Viv didn't train as hard then. He didn't have time to train because he was running all over the place. His mobile-phone number changed that many times because there were that many people who had his number.'

What about Higgins Security, from Birmingham, who were apparently employed to get Viv out of a pub he was running? Is this true? 'They phoned Viv up and asked to meet him and he met them and took them for dinner. They actually wanted Viv to work for them, the Higgins Security Company.'

Weren't they called in though by a North-East pub, a Newcastle pub? Peter looked puzzled and said, 'To stop Viv from entry? They couldn't stop Viv from entry. I knew that he had a meeting and had to go to Birmingham, but he didn't go.'

I recalled a story I was told, which was that Viv had slapped one of the Higgins crew around and they all left after giving

Viv some money. Another story was that a publican called in Higgins Security because Viv was causing some trouble. They went to see Viv and told him not to go into the pub and Viv complied. When Peter was asked if this was true, he told me, 'Viv wouldn't go down [to Birmingham]. They offered to take him for a meal and meet him and obviously give him a bite of the cherry. They knew he was the only one up here who could control the doors.'

Peter related how Higgins Security men were controlling the doors of certain places in Newcastle. The men working for such a lucrative company had to abide by the company's wishes, but they were scared while on Tyneside.

Peter said, 'The guys were frightened on those doors, even though Higgins was the company. They were frightened they had to do it. Everybody was going to stick by them if there was a fight. Whoever got hit got hit. In Viv's case, they tried to befriend him because they didn't want to get on Viv's bad side.

'It was costing them a lot of money to bring these people up from Birmingham and keeping them in hotels. It was costing them a lot more money than what Viv was getting.

'I think it was the fact that there was that many getting in for nothing in some of the clubs was the reason the security company was called in. They started off in some of the clubs, as well as some of the nightclubs; they seemed to get bigger and bigger.

'You could see that they wanted nothing to do with Viv when he went to the places. You could see that the fear of the thought of him coming to the places put the fear of God into them. There was never any trouble. Viv didn't cause trouble for the sake of causing trouble.'

When the name Manny Burgo was brought up, Peter said, 'Another thing that was said about Manny Burgo was what he was supposed to do to Viv in the ring. Manny was around in the amateur boxing scene the same time as Viv.

'I saw Manny back away from him. When Viv caught him, he couldn't get out, he shouted, "Viv! I've come to sort it out." Manny was more or less in charge of the coast. He didn't ever venture on to Viv's territory, but then obviously Viv got well known.

'It didn't stop here; it was getting bigger and bigger, so eventually these people were getting sick of the people they had paid for a long time and they wanted Viv; it was as simple as that. People would say, "Who's he?" And just about everyone knew him, "They call him Viv," would be the reply.

'Then he started going into Whitley Bay, Tynemouth, and he started getting bigger pubs and clubs. They felt he shouldn't be doing this because he was cutting them out of a job. Viv would say, "I'll keep two of your pubs and you can have the rest yourselves." Manny Burgo had come into Newcastle to see Viv to sort the situation out.'

Peter continued, 'In Macey's, there was him [Manny] and a few of his pals, and he had come to try and see Viv. There was something or another said. You've never seen anybody run! Viv was running this way and the other to try and catch him! Manny talked his way out of it and Viv gave him the benefit of the doubt and didn't hit him or anything, and this man Burgo is huge.

'Manny actually got in the car to drop me off. It was never mentioned again. When Manny ever sees me now, he never speaks or anything, he just walks straight past, and, mind, I watched him box, but I never rated him. He didn't ever fear me in any way and I wasn't feared of him. I'm not feared of anyone that I've mentioned, I don't fear for Adam.'

Peter didn't think people like this had made Viv into what he was. 'He had to be Viv Graham on his own. He couldn't be Viv Graham with Billy Robinson or Paddy Leonard. I think you start to meet new people and new friends. I don't think Viv ever thought to any extreme that things were going to come to him: he being wanted as badly by different pubs and clubs and even shops.'

16
RUSSIAN ROULETTE

There are two stories of how Duffy met his death. I'll give you the one some of you may have read in the hundreds of column inches of newspaper articles and features that have been written about it. I do not intend to rehash those features, so I will move through it as quickly as possible. What follows is the official version of events and, as we know, 'official' versions differ a great deal from 'real-life' events.

25 August 1991: David James Allison killed Lee Paul Duffy at 3.30am outside the Afro-West Caribbean Centre, in Marton Road, Middlesbrough. After what is claimed to have been an argument in the centre, both men became embroiled in a fight outside.

February 1993: Allison, 26, of Overfields, Teesside, faced a packed court, where he claimed he feared Duffy might have a gun when the pair fought and that he swung out with a knife that was handed to him during the fight because he was frightened Duffy was going to kill him.

Allison said that he'd seen Duffy with a gun on previous occasions. Once Duffy, Allison claimed, pulled out a gun and did not say or do anything. He believed Duffy was playing mind games with him.

At the trial, the jury heard that Allison had told police, 'I had to fight on; I was fighting for my life.' Allison and Duffy had clashed several times in the past, and on one occasion Allison had been given a good hiding by Duffy in Blazes nightclub, in Middlesbrough.

In the Afro-West Caribbean Centre, Duffy offered to fight Allison, who, not wanting to appear a coward, accepted. Allison claimed Duffy said to him, 'I'm going to bust your head in and kill you.' After that they started fighting and Duffy overpowered Allison, who said, 'I thought my head was going to split again. I thought he was going to kill me.'

Allison broke free and he was handed a knife. In his own words, 'He came lunging at me; I was exhausted at the time and just swung out with it. He backed off, saying, "I'm going to kill you, you've stabbed me."

'I used the knife to protect myself, to hurt him, to win the fight. If not, he would have come after me, used a knife or used a gun.'

Self-defence is the 'minimum' use of force required to defend yourself or your property from the real threat of an injury or further injury or even death.

Allison told the court that he was in the wrong place at the wrong time when Lee Duffy decided to pick a fight with him. Giving evidence in his own defence, he added, 'He put his hand round the back of my neck. I thought about the knuckleduster in my pocket. I thought to hit him with it.

Finish it at that and leave. I thought I might knock him unconscious. I would have to leave him unconscious to be able to walk away.

'I believed he could kill a person ... he was capable of it. He started to beat me up. He came forward at me and threw me to the ground. I landed on my back. Duffy got on top of me. He was braying my head off the floor.

'I thought he was going to kill me, I thought my head was going to split open. The knuckleduster was in my right hand. I was hitting the back of his head, trying to get him off me. He was butting me. I bit his cheek. I heard someone say, "Shiv him!" I now know that means to stab someone.

'Then, for some reason, he was off me. I was helped to my feet by some friends and taken to a nearby wall. When I was against the wall, the knife was put in my hand. Someone said, "Protect yourself!"

'I could hardly walk. I did not know where I was. I just wanted to get away from him and go home. I was terrified and semi-conscious. I could not let myself go unconscious. He would have killed me there and then. I took him seriously when he said he was going to kill me.

'Some people were shouting, "He's got a gun!" I was terrified. I was confused. Duffy came towards me. He had an object in his hand. I don't know what it was. When he walked forward, he raised it. I thought it might be a gun.

'There was nowhere to run. I was not in a fit state to run. I walked forward to get on to Marton Road and go home. He raised his arm, so I lashed out. I did not aim for any part of his body. I did not intend to kill him. I did not want to cause him serious harm. All I wanted was for him to leave me alone.'

Later that morning Allison visited Middlesbrough General Hospital, where he learned the shocking news that Duffy was dead.

The court was told by Allison that he had met Lee King and Richard Neil for drinks at a pub in Middlesbrough town centre and then they went on to the blues party, getting there shortly before Duffy arrived with some Geordie friends. Allison later described them as 'gangsters'.

James Spencer QC, the prosecutor at the murder trial, which took place nearly 18 months after Duffy's death, said, 'Allison had been drinking for 12 hours before the fight, while Duffy, known as Teesside's top dog, had taken Ecstasy tablets and cocaine.

'Seconds representing each man had separated the pair into corners and, when round one came to an end, they had a minute's rest.'

During the fight Allison wore a knuckleduster and used this to his advantage, and, when Duffy spotted metal in his hand, he said, 'You cannot even do it with metal in your hand.'

In defence of Allison's actions, David Robson QC told the court that his client was trapped in the car park and, believing Duffy was armed with a revolver, acted only in self-defence. 'He was like an animal in a cage; if there was an evil supreme in Middlesbrough, it was Lee Duffy. Allison was the rabbit in the trap.'

David Woodier, a prosecution witness, told the jury that Duffy had punched him senseless for no good reason two weeks before his death.

The jury was given a graphic description of Duffy's last minutes. Woodier went on to say, 'Duffy enjoyed the fear people had of him.' Maybe he should have been a defence witness.

He went on to describe how Duffy had entered the Afro-West Caribbean Centre looking 'stoned and wild-eyed', and he agreed with the defence QC, David Robson, that Duffy had 'poisoned the atmosphere' of the previously jovial and happy place.

Duffy was supposed to have entered the club telling people to 'move' and 'get out of my way, now!'. Woodier went on to say that he could sense something was going to happen and that Duffy had approached Allison and said, 'Do people think we are going to fight?' Then he saw Duffy walk outside and Allison follow him.

Woodier said he went out about five minutes later and described how Duffy and Allison had hold of each other in a sort of lock. 'I noticed Lee had his top off and was bare-chested. David Allison was covered in blood. Both seemed to let go of each other at the same time. Allison looked tired and worn out. At that stage Duffy was jumping about looking really fit, like a boxer.

'I heard Duffy say to Allison, "You had to use a knuckleduster, but you still couldn't put me away." Allison answered, "When it comes to bullies like you, I have to use something." Duffy seemed to get very angry. He picked up a bottle off the wall and said, "You know what I'm going to do, don't you?"

'Duffy brought one of his arms round holding the bottle. Allison seemed to move to one side and pointed his arm out in a sort of roundhouse move. Duffy was facing him. That blow struck Duffy towards his left arm.

'Straight away Duffy put his arm across his chest and said, "Get me to hospital, I'm dead." There was blood, a lot of blood! I saw his jeans turn red.'

David Robson QC asked Woodier some questions.

Robson: 'Allison did not go out to terrorise people in the way Duffy did?'

Woodier: 'No.'

Robson: 'Lee Duffy had the town terrified, didn't he?'

Woodier: 'Yes.'

I cannot understand what the prosecution were doing in using Woodier as a witness, as he did nothing other than help the defence.

Alongside Allison were Richard Ralph Neil, 20, charged with assisting Allison to get away from the scene, and Lee Robert King, 25, charged with attempting to pervert the course of justice by dropping the knife down a drain. Both men denied the charges.

During the course of the trial various witnesses who were friends of either Duffy or Allison gave evidence. Duffy's friend John Fail told the court, 'Allison was staggering after Duffy had banged his head on the ground and nutted him several times.'

Adrian Boddy, an acquaintance of Allison, recalled, 'At one stage Duffy picked Allison up in a rugby tackle and smashed him to the floor. Allison just stood there staggering, I never saw anything in his hand. Allison had swung several punches at Duffy, but failed to make any contact.

'It was after one blow which did land under Duffy's armpit that Duffy shouted he was dying.'

On behalf of the police, Dr Alistair Irvine, a police surgeon, examined Allison after the fight and confirmed that the injuries he had received were consistent with having spent some time on his back during the fight and that the injuries to his head were consistent with its having been banged on the ground several times.

Dr Irvine also testified that there were also indications of blows to his face.

Questioned by the judge, Angus Stroyan QC, Dr Irvine confirmed that such blows could have caused a concussional effect and would have caused a significant jarring effect to the head.

The Home Office pathologist, Dr John McCarthy, described Duffy's injuries, which included two stab wounds: one to the back, which did not prove, nor could have proved, fatal; and one to his armpit, which severed an axillary (main) artery, causing Duffy to bleed to death within minutes. (The stab wound to Duffy's back is considered below.)

A telephone call at 8am alerted David James Allison Snr to the incident involving his son and Lee Duffy. In a phone call to his father, Allison said, 'I think I've killed Lee Duffy!'

When Allison pleaded with his father to get his clothes from a garage rooftop, he agreed to do that.

David Allison Snr appeared on behalf of the prosecution and he told the court that his son was crying when he telephoned him and he told his son to give himself up to the police.

Allison, a scaffolder, rang his father again at 11.30am, saying he would give himself up at his aunt's house.

The reason Allison gave the court for having a knuckleduster in his possession was that Duffy had threatened him the day before the fatal stabbing. Prior to that, the knuckleduster had sat at his mother's home for some years.

As mentioned earlier, Allison claimed that someone shouted that Duffy had a gun, and it was claimed that Duffy had held something aloft in his hand and that Allison may have been concussed.

An exhibit was produced in court, namely a Smith and Wesson .38 revolver, said to have been found near the scene of Duffy's fatal stabbing!

Blues party DJ Saidhu Kamara told the court how a gun 'fell' from a black leather jacket that he found near his DJ box at the Afro-West Caribbean Centre after the fatal fight. The jacket, he said, was 'similar' to one that Duffy had been wearing earlier that evening.

After finding the gun, Kamara said, he had hidden it in a nearby derelict house and later buried it beneath a rosebush at his girlfriend's home.

Joseph Livingstone, a friend of Allison, found out about this hidden gun that was buried beneath a rosebush. Livingstone approached Kamara, saying that the solicitor representing Allison, James Watson, would like to see the item in order to help with his defence at the trial.

A forensic scientist, Michael Hammond, gave testimony to the court that Duffy had consumed a massive amount of Ecstasy and that blood samples taken from his body had revealed a high concentration of metabolised cocaine and traces of alcohol.

Mr Hammond went on to say that the amount of Ecstasy in Duffy's body was two micrograms per millilitre, which is an extremely high level of the drug, and, in some cases, that concentration could be life-threatening.

The court was further told by Mr Hammond that high doses of Ecstasy could produce anxiety, paranoia, symptoms of psychosis, together with mood swings and violent irritability. He advised that cocaine could have a similar effect, including causing aggressive behaviour. The combination of the two drugs would make each more effective than one on its own.

A host of witnesses were brought forward to testify to Duffy's gun-toting exploits. It was stated that he:

- Once held a gun to taxi driver Arzur Shan's head in a bizarre game of Russian roulette. He spun the chamber after putting one bullet into it and fired at the taxi driver's head while ordering him to drive faster, but the gun never went off. He then pulled the gun away and fired it again, and this time the gun went off, making a hole through the taxi's roof. This was done to impress someone who was with him.

- Often played a game of one-man Russian Roulette in front of Karen Pitelem at her home in Thornaby with a revolver loaded with one bullet. He would say, and believe, that he was 'invincible' before pulling the trigger a number of times as he held the gun to his head.

- Played three-man Russian Roulette with friends. One man 'bottled out' and, on the third pull of the trigger, with Duffy pointing the gun at the wall, the weapon fired a bullet.

- Asked a DJ in a nightclub to dedicate a record to David

Allison and continually waved a gun at him while the record played.

- Fired a gun into the wall of Karen Pitelem's house when visiting as an unwanted guest, in order to frighten her.
- Fired a gun in the Havana nightclub in Middlesbrough.

However, forensic evidence showed that Duffy had *not* been in contact with a gun on the night of his death.

Duffy had earlier assaulted a man who would try to save his life. In an unprovoked attack by Duffy, Stephen Pearson had been thrown backwards and grabbed by the throat. Later, Pearson saw the fight leading up to the stabbing and chased after the fatally wounded Duffy as he ran in various directions shouting for help.

Mr Pearson took off his T-shirt and used it to try to stem the blood spouting from the wound to Duffy's armpit. He tied a tourniquet and helped place the mortally wounded Duffy into a car that had been flagged down. Immediately before this, an attempt had been made to flag down a taxi, but it had sped off.

When it was Lee King's turn to be represented, his defence counsel, Jamie Hill, told the jury that they had to be sure that King had intended to pervert the course of justice when he disposed of the knife.

Mr Hill said, 'He had just seen his friend Allison having his head pounded on the floor and suffering considerable injuries at the hands of Duffy. It must have been a fairly fraught experience for Lee King. He must have been fairly shocked.'

Earlier, Richard Neil had pleaded guilty to unlawful possession of the lock knife, but he too denied assisting an offender. 'There is not a shred of evidence that what Neil was doing was assisting an offender,' his counsel, Ian West, told the jury.

King was found guilty of attempting to pervert the course of justice as a consequence of trying to hide the killer lock knife by dropping it down a drain. Charges against both Neil and King of assisting an offender were dismissed. King received 150 hours' community service for hiding the knife. He had previously been jailed for 18 months for assaulting an off-duty policeman.

Allison was acquitted of murder and walked from the court a free man. He had punched the air when a verdict of 'not guilty' was returned after two hours of deliberation at the end of an eight-day trial. He said, 'I'm all right. I'm not sad about the verdict anyway.'

Lisa Stockell, Duffy's last long-term girlfriend, said that she thought that too much of Duffy's past was brought up in the trial and that Duffy's character was repeatedly attacked.

Duffy's mother, Brenda, and Lisa both burst into tears when they heard the verdict. Brenda Duffy said, 'Lee would not have wanted this man to go down.'

Some claimed that Duffy led a charmed life in being able to avoid so many attempts on his life, but, in reality, it was Duffy's upbringing that helped him survive these attacks. An unremitting tirade of attacks had caused countless injuries to his body, which was riddled with lead shot. Was this a charmed life?

Viv Graham needed to be just as vigilant in the face of attacks, but he was not. With Duffy, it was only a matter of time before he was killed. Viv had fewer assassination attempts to contend with, but his lack of survival instinct was his Achilles heel.

A man like Duffy parading around Tyneside would have been a force to be reckoned with, and had he teamed up with Viv, as he did with the big fella from Teesside, Brian Cockerill, for a short period, maybe he would have had the whole of the North sewn up.

The kingdoms of Viv Graham and Lee Duffy have since been broken up into smaller estates, run by lesser mortals than Viv and the Duffer. Factions that keep a low profile find safety in numbers. No longer is there a big name for them to rely on as a weapon of defence.

Since the days of the Duffer, the incidence of violence has actually increased regionally and nationally.

17
NO MORE GOOD TIMES

The account of the events leading to Lee Duffy's death given in the previous chapter is based on fact. We add some further insights which should make the whole of the moon visible to you. 'The Whole of the Moon', by the Waterboys, was Duffy's favourite song.

Confirmation was sought that there was indeed an ongoing conflict between Duffy and Allison. In fact, there was a conflict between Allison (nicknamed 'Allo') and Duffy. At the wedding of a mutual friend called John Graham, Duffy and Allo had a bit of a set-to, but nothing ferocious. Years earlier they had had a fight and, according to some, they had repeated skirmishes.

One night Duffy was in the Havana when he met up with some friends from Hartlepool. They were ferried by taxis to a blues party in Princes Road, Middlesbrough, where the first attempt on Duffy's life had taken place some eight months earlier. From there they went on to the Afro-West Caribbean

Centre in Marton Road around 3.15am. Fifteen minutes later Duffy would be dead.

Outside the centre stood Stephen 'Morph' Reed, roaringly drunk. He was put into a cab and sent home by one of Duffy's party. It seemed that this night was to have a calamitous effect on many of the people present, as if something sinister pervaded the place.

That night in the centre, a man called Fields had given a letter to someone to pass on to Allo.

It was claimed that the man approached Allo, who was up against the back wall, and was seen to pass him the letter. On seeing the man approach Allo, Duffy went over and said to him 'What the fuck are you talking to that rat for?'

At this point Allo looked like a frightened mouse. After Duffy and Allo went outside, the doors were shut behind them. At first nobody saw what happened. They tell you this, they tell you that, but nobody other than the few present from both sides saw anything that happened. Apart, that is, from a third party who has spoken to me. What follows is based on the information he supplied.

Duffy grabbed him, threw him to the ground like a rag doll and straddled him. Allo received numerous headbutts and then had his head smashed against the ground by Duffy.

The Duffer then started to pull Allo's head towards him to headbutt him again. Wearing a knuckleduster, Allo was trying to bring his hand over the top to hit Duffy.

This fits in exactly with Allison's testimony in court: 'Then, for some reason, he was off me. I was helped to my feet by some friends and taken to a nearby wall.'

The fight was broken up, though at first no one would act

to do that. One of Duffy's lieutenants slipped in between Allo and Duffy, put his arms tightly around Duffy's midriff and pulled him up, using a movement not unlike the Heimlich manoeuvre, which is applied when someone is choking on something stuck in their throat.

Remember, Duffy had been shot twice some months before this and he had a bad limp owing to the state of his knee and foot, each damaged in separate attempts on his life.

Next, Duffy sat on a wall and Allo then went straight for him. During the course of the ensuing struggle and as the jury subsequently confirmed, acting in self defence, Allo did a roundhouse move. After a further scuffle, Duffy brought his hand to a main artery.

Immediately, Duffy put his arm down by his side and said, 'Fucking hell, Allo, you've killed me. This one's serious.'

Duffy turned to run. He ran just 20 or so yards from the scene, shouting for help, before collapsing on the road. A big fight took place; everyone ran off, leaving Duffy nearby on the ground, still alive. In a previous book, it was mistakenly stated that it was Peter Donnelly who was in the taxi with Duffy when he went to hospital, but it is now known that this was not the case.

What had happened was, Duffy had brought a group of Geordies into town and the locals were saying they were 'Geordie Gangsters' and the 'Geordie Mafia'. The situation was like a timebomb. But, once the kingpin, Duffy, was taken out, the locals did not give two hoots about the Geordie Mafia; it didn't matter who they were, because they were from out of town.

The minute Duffy was taken out of the equation, the locals steamed into his group. There were about 20 people fighting in the street. The Geordie Mafia, without their main piece of artillery, Duffy, got a good kicking.

At this point Duffy was sitting up in the street shouting for help, his lifeblood pumping out of him like a fountain, and as it hit the ground it made a clapping sound. 'Help me, someone help me,' he was calling out. By this time a crowd had gathered around Duffy and shouts of 'Die' were heard.

A taxi came in to view but, seeing people trying to flag it down, the driver promptly did a U-turn and left the scene. He has not been traced. It can only be hoped he is not a reflection of what taxi drivers are like in Middlesbrough.

A passing car was stopped, driven by John Smith – his real name – and it is clear that the man who flagged it down was Mark Hartley. By now Duffy was lying face down and in a state of shock with scarlet blood squirting feet high into the early-morning air.

Whatever Hartley said to the driver, it worked, as he allowed him to put Duffy in the back of the car. As Hartley struggled to get Duffy off the ground, a crowd of some few hundred had gathered, as if watching some gruesome horror show. One gallant person, Stephen Pearson, stepped forward from the morbid crowd and said he would help.

He freely admitted that he did not like Duffy, but he still helped. Many are called but few are chosen. Hartley took hold of Duffy's upper body, while Pearson took hold of his legs and they put him into the back of John Smith's Ford Escort. Duffy's head was behind the driver and his feet were bent up across the back seat. Hartley jumped into the front passenger seat, along with another man who ran and leaped in to get away from a man he had earlier been fighting with.

Hartley was perched on the obstructive passenger's knees in the front of the car and leaned across to tend to Duffy, who, by all accounts, was still alive.

The driver set off to hospital as fast as he could and, as the car went through the hospital gates, Duffy took his last gasp and is believed to have died.

The paramedics went through the motions and applied electric shock to stimulate Duffy's heart back to life. An hour or two later, it is claimed, Peter Donnelly and another two Geordies turned up at the hospital.

Lisa, Duffy's girlfriend, was called on the phone and she says that Mark Hartley told her that Lee had been stabbed. When she asked how bad it was, Hartley is said to have told her that he didn't know.

Lisa, her mother and her stepfather, Terry, turned up at the hospital and there they saw the lone figure of Mark Hartley outside the casualty department.

Lisa ran up to him screaming, '*I want to know, I want t o know!*'

'He's dead, Lisa,' came the reply and, with that, Lisa became hysterical.

At 3.30am Duffy was killed. At 3.31am the police received a telephone call saying there had been a road traffic accident (which fits in with the fact that Duffy was lying in the road) and at 3.33am the police received a call saying Allison had killed Duffy.

The police were already aware of who was responsible for Duffy's death; they just wanted someone to finally finger him. In the end, Allison fingered himself.

The holding cells were to see the arrival of Allison at

2.20pm that afternoon and he was put only a few cells away from Hartley. Just yards apart, they could so easily have spoken to each other. This is often a ploy used by the police in the hope that, if their captives talk to each other, they might learn something.

In this connection, witness evidence gathered for this book is first class, so, should anyone think of pursuing a civil action against me, it's wise to remember that in such cases there is much less burden of proof needed to secure convictions resulting from civil evidence.

Yes, King had dumped the knife down a drain!

Since the advent of DNA evidence and improved forensic detection, it would seem a logical approach to make the court system just as fair for the families of murdered loved ones.

In an amazing series of coincidences it seems as if the lives of those surrounding Lee Duffy were fated.

Lee King was blasted to death on 28 January 2000. His body was discovered, in Penistone Road, Park End, Middlesbrough, with shotgun wounds to the head and back. Keith McQuade, 45, was remanded in custody in September 2000, some eight months after the murder investigation had begun.

The date of 5 February 2001 saw the start of the murder trial, in which King, 32, was described as a man with a reputation as a womaniser; this is an important fact to remember. McQuade denied the charge of murder and was subsequently acquitted.

'McQuade stuck a sawn-off shotgun into Mr King's back in a Teesside street in the early hours of the morning and blasted him through the heart at close range. As his rival lay wounded, McQuade reloaded and shot him in the head at close range,' said James Spencer QC, prosecuting.

The Prosecution alleged that King had a one-night stand with an ex-lover of McQuade, Lisa Piercey, 25. After this he called her a 'slut'. Mr Spencer said that McQuade had told a friend that Mr King had made a fool of him over the woman. McQuade said that King told him two nights before he was killed that he had slept with McQuade's former lover. McQuade told the court that King had said to him, 'You are not bothered about it, are you, because I was round there that night? She's a slut anyway, isn't she?' McQuade said he replied, 'She's got three kids to three different fellas. It's got nothing to do with me.'

Mr Spencer told the court that McQuade had said, 'He told me about sleeping with Lisa and said she was only a slut. I told him, "You don't need to do something like that to me," and I pointed the gun at him. He said, "You won't do something like that to me," and he walked away. I shot him once in the back and then in the head.'

It was alleged that McQuade had acted out the killing afterwards to two friends, telling them that King had turned his back on the gun, saying, 'You wouldn't dare!'

McQuade told the court that King had invited him to take part in an armed robbery on a crack house in Kensington Road, Middlesbrough, which was planned for the night King was killed. He went on to say that King had arrived at his lodgings in Kenilworth Avenue, Park End, to collect some tools he had hidden in the back garden. King then produced a sawn-off shotgun wrapped in bin liners, at which point McQuade told King that he wanted nothing to do with the robbery.

When King's body was found, he was clutching a knife in one hand and there was a bag containing two balaclavas. This was McQuade's defence: that it was King who had organised the proposed crack-house robbery.

They left the lodgings together and went in opposite directions and the next day McQuade heard that King had been shot dead. When asked why he thought witnesses had given evidence against him, McQuade told the court that he believed that prosecution witnesses were involved in drugs and had plotted with each other to tell lies.

A prosecution witness told the court that McQuade had left a friend's house carrying a holdall which is alleged to have held the sawn-off shotgun that was used to kill King. A mechanic, John Johnson, known as 'Car Jack', told the court that on 28 January 2000 he was working in his garage when his neighbour Peter Heeran walked in and said, 'Keith needs a lift, urgent.'

Johnson said he drove McQuade to a mutual friend's nearby home and, ten minutes later, on his return, he heard emergency-vehicle sirens. A while later, Heeran called into the garage and told Johnson that Lee King had been shot. Johnson went on to say, 'Heeran said to me, "It served him right, he was trying to get me shot." I told him that I did not want to know anything about it.'

In April 2001 the jury found McQuade not guilty of murdering King. Nearly to the exact day, in the same month, on the eighth anniversary of David Allison's acquittal of murdering Lee Duffy, Keith McQuade was acquitted of murdering Lee King.

King was shot in the back. It is claimed that King lay on the ground mortally wounded (just as Duffy did) before the next gunshot blasted him in the head. (Although it was also suggested that Duffy was also slashed on the right leg.)

A further twist in the tale is that the woman involved in this was called Lisa, the same name as Duffy's girlfriend, Lisa Stockell.

After McQuade was acquitted of King's murder, Detective Superintendent Adrian Roberts said, 'There is not a shred of evidence to implicate anyone else associated with the investigation, or to suggest a new inquiry. We will not be looking for anyone else.'

King was murdered on 28 January 2000. Two days later, Beverly Reynolds, 31, a mother of three, was found hanging by a piece of wire around her neck from a loft hatch ... she had killed herself.

Scaffolder David Allison, 32, found the body of his girlfriend, who had returned home on her own earlier after rowing with him during a night out in Middlesbrough. It is claimed that she wanted to stay out longer while Allison wanted to return home. In the event, Beverly returned home first, by taxi, after the row, and as she did not have a key she had to smash the glass of the door to get in. Her children were staying overnight with relatives, so when she entered the house she was alone.

At the inquest on Beverly Reynolds, held in January 2001, Dr Jeremiah Murphy spoke, he said he was treating Miss Reynolds for depression caused by domestic stress and said that she had twice taken overdoses of Paracetamol.

On 31 January 1991 two men had burst into the home of

Lisa Stockell and forced a gun into her mouth in order to find out where her boyfriend Lee Duffy was. Nine years almost to the day, on 30 January 2000, tragedy struck again, but this time against the man who had killed Duffy in self defence.

Now Allison had been put in the same position as lone parents Lisa Stockell and Carol 'Bonnie' Holmstrom, the women with whom Duffy had had children. Duffy's three children were fatherless and now the three children of Allison's girlfriend were motherless.

The devastation that this loss will have brought to Miss Reynolds's children is mind-numbing. Lisa Stockell and Carol Holmstrom were forced to come to terms with the loss of their children's father.

You might think it can get no worse, but it does! Beverly, Allo's girlfriend, was rumoured to be having an affair with Lee King and it was two days after King's death that she committed suicide. You have already read that she and Allison were arguing earlier that night and that she was being treated for depression due to domestic stress. It all got too much for Beverly and it is rumoured that she decided that, if King was taken away from her, then Allison would not have her.

When the police arrived at the tragic scene in Allison's home in the early hours of Sunday, it was PC Timothy Lowe, the first officer to enter the house in Ormesby, Teesside, who gave mouth-to-mouth resuscitation to Beverly.

PC Lowe told the inquest that he could hear Allison downstairs and he seemed very distressed. 'He became more and more agitated, passing from anger to violence. He went into the kitchen and smashed a chair and threw a radio-cassette into the sink. He kept throwing himself about the kitchen. He was saying, "Who will tell the kids? What am I going to do?" He caused damage to numerous items in the house.'

The coroner for Central Teesside, Michael Sheffield, recorded a verdict that Beverly killed herself.

Violence attracts violence and, as Duffy once said, 'Those who live by the sword die by the sword.' Further tragedy struck when Kevin Howard, who had once fought with Duffy, hanged himself.

Duffy also used to say, 'Treat good people good, treat bad people bad.' Many people saw him as a Jekyll and Hyde, but he was an adaptable person and has been described as speaking both the language of the street and the language of the jet set. Someone said cryptically, 'Duffy spoke 15 languages.' What was meant was that he could communicate in the language of violence or the language of business. You could take him to tea in an old people's home and he would be most respectful, but put him in a blues party and he acted accordingly. He wore his heart on his sleeve.

Investigations into when Duffy was shot in the first murder attempt at Princes Road revealed that this was carried out in a similar fashion to the way Viv was murdered. In Duffy's case, the hitmen stood in a dark alleyway and shouted to him to come over.

(In Viv's case, it was a car that was parked in a dark alleyway and from inside it they shouted something at Viv to attract his attention so as to get his body square on, to make a better target.)

Duffy, though, unlike Viv, had seen the gun that his would-be assassins carried. This is the difference between Duffy and Viv.

FIGHT TO THE DEATH

On seeing the gun, Duffy turned and went to run backwards, which, given his speed and power, would be as fast as some people could run forwards. He jumped behind a car and they opened fire, managing only to shoot him in the leg. Duffy had escaped death by the skin of his teeth. They were trying to take him out, and they were not giving him a warning!

The second attempt on Duffy's life by people who have never been identified, as you now know, was at an illegal blues party. As three men walked up to him he spotted them and tried to slip around them in the darkened room. He tried to work his way to the door but they caught him before he could get out. Duffy instinctively knew they were out to kill him.

One of them pulled a shotgun out of his long coat; Duffy instinctively grabbed the barrel of the shotgun and started fighting with his would-be killer. While he was trying to wrest the gun from him, one of the other two men had a crowbar and started hitting Duffy over the head in the hope that he would let go of the weapon.

To prove this is true, the records later showed that Duffy also had quite a few stitches put into the back of his head. At no time did any of the hired hitmen push the gun downwards – this was a full-blown hit meant to kill Duffy. While Duffy was fighting with the gun, one shot went off and missed, which again supports the shoot-to-kill theory.

When Duffy was in hospital, he had photographs in his possession of the so-called 'professional' hitmen, along with their names and addresses written on the back of each photo.

The Prosecution did not proceed against those accused in

this second murder attempt on Duffy's life because there was no evidence to implicate them. Two of the accused, Marnon Thomas and Leroy Fischer, made an unsuccessful attempt in 1999 to pursue Cleveland Police Force for compensation for 'malicious prosecution' in a High Court action. Both petitioners claimed damages from Cleveland Chief Constable Barry Shaw following their acquittal in 1991 of involvement in a conspiracy to shoot Lee Duffy.

Lawyers representing Birmingham men Thomas and Fischer called the Crown prosecutor for Teesside, Keith Simpson. Mr Simpson has denied being involved in any deal to grant immunity to Ria Nasir, of South Bank, Middlesbrough, one of the suspects. The High Court – sitting at Teesside – was told by Mr Simpson that any such deal would need approval at a much higher level than himself.

Nasir had been questioned in connection with the shooting by police treating the case as attempted murder when unsubstantiated intelligence reports suggested that some of the men involved in the shooting were seen at or near Nasir's home.

Teesside solicitor Keith Leigh, who represented Nasir at the time, had told the High Court that he had been involved in 'striking a bargain' with Detective Superintendent Len Miller, with the aim of having all charges against her dropped if she cooperated with police investigating the shooting. Mr Leigh claimed Mr Simpson was present for part of these discussions.

Nasir's lawyer also claimed he witnessed her – who he said had a drink problem – being interviewed by officers in Middlesbrough Police Station while under the influence of drink, drinking brandy and with a bottle of brandy close at hand. He told the court, 'She was not being interviewed under caution, she was not at risk. I was perfectly happy to let the police conduct the investigation as they saw fit.'

Mr Simpson told the court that all he had done was to offer the police advice. He said, 'I was there to advise the police about the prosecution rather than the investigation.'

He had recommended no action against Nasir on the basis that the only evidence was an informal, unrecorded conversation between her and the then Detective Inspector Ray Mallon and this could not have produced a realistic prospect of convicting Nasir on charges relating to the shooting.

Cross-examined by barrister Peter Johnson, for the Chief Constable, Mr Simpson said that on the evidence submitted by the police to the CPS – which included that of Nasir – he was satisfied that the charges brought against Thomas, Fischer and others were 'appropriate'.

Both Marnon Thomas and Leroy Fischer lost their case for a frivolous claim when Judge Michael Taylor said, 'Whatever shortcomings in the investigation that the case had thrown up – they did not affect the central issue of malice. The claimants had maintained they had been wrongly prosecuted as a result of identification evidence provided in a deal struck between police and South Bank woman Ria Nasir at a time when she was herself a suspect in the case and known to be "unreliable" as a witness.'

Judge Taylor gave judgment in favour of the police and said the decision by Detective Superintendent Len Miller to drop potential charges against Nasir in exchange for information from her was a 'totally justifiable' gamble, taken at a time when the investigation was 'up against the buffers'.

The judge also said 'It was clear that those directly

involved in the shooting were from outside Teesside. With almost all the potential witnesses coming from the criminal community, there was little chance of co-operation in finding out their identities.'

Judge Taylor added that it was in the public interest to have convicted several people prepared to use a shotgun in a public place rather than have one woman in the dock.

Fischer, who at that time was serving a five-year sentence for robbery, started shouting abuse at the judge and police officers in the court and continued as he was led away to the cells.

Chief Superintendent Miller was delighted with the outcome and said, 'I'm pleased the judge supported our decision to take a risk in an effort to catch the people responsible for the shooting.'

In a prison letter Duffy wrote:

'Manny Burgo [the boxer] was in the blues last weekend, Allo and some lads were working themselves with Manny, so he knocked 3 or 4 of them out, or so I have been told. (Hope it wasn't Allo.)'

Another of Duffy's letters, dated April 1991 and written from HM Prison Durham, says:

'Lee Harrison has been up to see me, well he actually done my head in, teasing me about the Havana, etc. He was at the courts yesterday taking the piss out of the police and generally making a disturbance, you know what he's like, he makes me laugh, he's off his head. I know this is going to sound daft but in a way I have been glad of the break from it all really. Living too fast, too long, it burns you out. But I could think of a better place to take a break like. (Ha, Ha.) But having said that I've had some brilliant times with you and the lads and I wouldn't change my lifestyle if it meant no more good times like we've had.'

To close this chapter, verdicts on the Teesside Terminator from both sides of the fence. First, Tommy Harrison:

'When Lee was fighting with Allo, that wasn't Lee fighting, he was as high as a kite, he was drunk, they were on champagne, Russian Blacks, and he hadn't been to bed for two days. He'd been on charley [cocaine] and his reflexes were gone. I don't think that would have happened if he wasn't under the influence of drink and drugs.'

Detective Chief Inspector Brian Leonard:

'There is always someone trying to put their head up and take the place of someone like Lee Duffy because they have seen him get away with it so much. But if there is a lesson to be learned it is this: if you get involved in drugs, violence and bullying you may come to a sticky end.'

Detective Sergeant Ray Morton:

'It is the end of an era. Many people have tried to emulate Lee Duffy, but they failed.'

18
'VIV NO MORE '94'

Viv left the Queen's Head pub in Wallsend at 6.05pm on New Year's Eve 1993. He was making the short walk back to where his powerful Ford Sierra Cosworth was parked in Border Road. The 'Cossie' had become his pride and joy when he replaced his BMW with it. It was a self-bestowed award that reflected his near-celebrity status.

The boy from Rowlands Gill had almost made it, and here was the proof. The metallic burgundy Cosworth reflected the sodium streetlights from its gleaming paintwork. A lone toy monkey hung from the rear-view mirror, like a talisman warding off evil.

The cigarettes and dog food that Viv had just bought from the corner shop, and carried in his brawny hands, signified the things he loved in his life: the cigarettes for his fiancée, whom he worshipped, and the dog food represented his love of animals. Here he was on New Year's Eve, thinking of the ones he loved and on his way back home to them.

Viv wished the shopkeeper 'Happy New Year' and they shook hands. There would be no late-night revelling for him because his fiancée, Anna Connelly, was not feeling well. She had stayed home, knowing her beloved Viv would soon be resting in his favourite position, with his feet up on the couch, among those he loved, with the phone off the hook and a video playing. Beneath this picture of serenity, there were some complicated issues in Viv's demanding life.

Conflicting thoughts may have been going through his head. He had just received a death threat by phone while he was in a pub passing time with friends and acquaintances. 'It's for you, Viv,' said the manager of the New Anchor as he handed him the phone.

'I've just had a death threat,' Viv said nonchalantly, keeping his innermost fears hidden – it did not do to show this lot his real self. Yet a part of his fear shone through like a shaft of light piercing a hole in a dark cloud on a sunny day. A few of those present had caught a glimpse of what they thought was a slight change in Viv's composure, but it would not have been wise to let him know they could see this.

Viv was the man, and no one messed with him. There was no one capable of doing him and, anyway, he was always getting death threats. This one was probably just from some upstart waging war over the phone because they knew they could do nothing to him in a one-to-one fight. What did Viv have to fear? These threats, after all, were ten a penny and it was probably just another wind-up, like all the previous threats had been. As far as Viv was concerned, it sucked.

Besides, Viv had more important things on his mind. He had just telephoned his secret lover, Gillian Lowes, and he told her he would be calling her at midnight to wish her a Happy New Year. There was not a day that went by when he did not have her or their two children on his mind.

It was a busy time of year and he would be in demand as usual, as there was always some troublemaker ready to cause upset at the drop of a hat. Viv was on call 24 hours a day, 365 days of the year.

Complacency has to come into it somewhere. Whereas at one time he was sensitive to his own security, now he had become too relaxed and lethargic where his personal safety was concerned. He had forgotten the lesson that he was taught in 1989 when he was shot at outside Manhattan's nightclub. This, as well as the trouble he had in Santino's restaurant, should have kept him on his toes. All forgotten! Watching too many videos may have created his current vision of being executed gangland style by a motorcyclist riding alongside his car.

Alarm bells should have started ringing when he received that threatening phone call. The thought of something happening must have given him a brief shock, but he had faced this before and his adrenalin just did not pump like it used to do at the beginning of his career.

Viv could camouflage his feelings and, anyway, it was soon masked by all the other thoughts of what he had to do, becoming just a haze in his mind. Tomorrow he would be seeing Gillian and his kids. This seemed more important to him than thinking of when a strike would happen against his life. 'Live for today' was his motto.

FIGHT TO THE DEATH

This was a time of year to relax and hang out with friends, and that is what Viv was doing. He had been in the Anchor since 4.15pm.

Fancying a change, he walked a few yards to the Queen's Head, where he stayed until 6.05pm, and on leaving there he called into a corner shop. People were making their way to a nearby bingo hall. Soon he would be cocooned in the womb-like safety of his beloved Cosworth and be back home in a flash with his devoted Anna; she would soothe away his stressed-out headache.

Within a few seconds of leaving the shop, Viv was at the side of his car, the keys in his hand. It was dark. As we know from Viv's father, Viv's was afraid of the dark! He was now in sight of his would-be killers. Accounts vary: at first it was said there were two of them, but later it was thought to be three.

Something to Viv did not look right, but he could not quite decide what it was; his mind was not thinking as straight as it normally did. That was it: the window on the car door was smashed. Oh no, not the broken-window diversion technique! A car pulled out from the nearby dark alley; something was called out to Viv! In a conditioned reflex, he turned to look.

BLAMH! Bullet number one was fired from a range of only five yards as the .357 Magnum handgun blasted out the first of three bullets. A flash, followed by a fiery pain milliseconds later, was the first indication to Viv that he had been shot. By its eerie echo, the noise had telegraphed to those in earshot that something ominous was going on.

Viv's instinctive reactions were swift. Before the first bullet had completed its journey through his thigh, having entered from the outside, his hand shot down so fast between his thighs that it beat the bullet exiting the leg. The bullet nicked the edge of his hand before continuing its blood-splattering route into the inside of his other thigh and out through the outside. Viv's legs were no longer responding to what his brain told them to do!

BLAMH! Bullet number two ripped apart Viv's lower abdominal area before emerging through his side, leaving organs in his muscled torso damaged beyond repair. The haemorrhaging was so bad that nothing in the long term would have saved Viv. A hole the size of a melon was visible in his side.

BLAMH! Bullet number three was fired at Viv when he was down; it had not fully made contact with him. The bullet, it is believed, may have ricocheted off the ground and fizzed over Viv's back, leaving a visible line. This was not a shoot-to-maim attack; it was clearly a shoot-to-kill attack. Had it been intended just to wound, once Viv had been put down by the first shot, that would have been that. But it was not: they shot again and again. And then drove off at a frantic pace.

Viv summoned up what was left of his strength and started to crawl back towards Wallsend High Street, which he had left just seconds earlier. The shopkeeper ran out to see what was going on. The injuries, obvious to the shopkeeper, who wished to remain anonymous, showed that the bullets had passed straight through Viv, leaving open wounds that were unmistakably caused by bullets.

Twenty-five yards away was the Queen's Head. Blind instinct must have been the only thing driving Viv on and leading him back the way he had come. Only this time, it was a crawling, bleeding, dying Viv that was seen through the window of the pub by Terry Scott, one of his associates. Terry ran out to Viv without concern for his own safety, although, unknown to him, the two killers had left the area when they sped off in the stolen blue Ford Escort.

As Viv lay there bleeding, he pulled his shirt down over his main wound in one last act of neatness.

'I can't let them see me like this,' he said. 'Terry, I'm going, I'm going.' Terry leaned his tall, powerful body over Viv to help him up to his feet; he could see there was a lot of damage to his body, but he could do little to help. He cradled Viv's head for a while; what a sight that must have been as Viv gasped, 'One last fight.'

Awake! For morning in the Bowl of Night
Has flung the stone that puts the stars to flight:
And Lo! The hunter of the East has caught
The Sultan's Turret in a noose of Light

Dreaming when Dawn's Left Hand was in the Sky,
I heard a voice within the Tavern cry,
'Awake, my little ones, and fill the cup
Before Life's Liquor in its Cup be dry.'

And as the Cock crew, those who stood before
The Tavern shouted – 'Open then the Door!
You know how little while we have to stay,
And once departed, may return no more.'
Now the New Year reviving old Desires,
The thoughtful Soul to solitude retires.

From *The Rubaiyat of Omar Khayyam*

When Peter Connelly arrived at the hospital, the scene that greeted him must have looked like bedlam. He was visibly moved by the amount of people he saw.

Terry Scott was running around venting his anger on the walls with punches that would have floored Mike Tyson.

Anna Connelly, Viv's fiancée, managed to see Viv briefly, and he said he loved her.

The doctor knew there was no hope. Viv could not survive the gaping hole in his side.

Jack Graham, Viv's father, said to Anna that his son would pull through, but Anna knew, seeing the severity of the visible damage, that the appalling wound would not allow him to continue living. It was to be the end of Viv's chaotic life.

Viv suffered a massive heart attack. How could the doctor tell a highly agitated group of relations, friends and associates who packed out the hospital waiting area that the man they had all willed to live was dead? Viv's body was placed in the recovery room, where, in death, he still looked quite normal. At 10.20 that night, when things had calmed down, Viv was pronounced dead after being formally identified by his father, although in fact he had died some hours earlier.

The unlit blue Ford Escort, registration number G668 DTF, had been in the area for a while before finally being dumped in Simonside Terrace, Heaton, Newcastle. Some 10 to 15 minutes after the murder, the car was torched. A later report was that a woman had nearly been knocked over by a blue Ford Escort in Debdon Gardens, only a minute's drive from Simonside Terrace.

Detective Superintendent John May, now retired, was in charge of the murder investigation. There were two independent witnesses to the incident, and both put a blonde woman as being on the other side of the main road and then, after Viv was shot, she was put as being near his body as she crossed the road towards the corner shop.

The getaway car had been stolen earlier in the day from Durham Road, Birtley, near Chester-le-Street, between 2.30pm and 3.30pm. It was also discovered that telephone calls were made to Viv's home that day asking where he was, and similar calls were made to the two pubs he had visited that day.

The word soon spread around Newcastle that Viv was dead. In certain quarters, champagne bottles popped their corks and the toast was: 'Viv no more '94.' Doormen refused to work, as they feared that they would be next on the hit list. The nightlife of the whole city came to an abrupt stop as doormen walked out in fear or sympathy.

The police made a number of what they believed to be key arrests: of Darren Arnold, Karen Young and her father, Brian William Tait, Alan Jackson, Alan Wheat, Michael Sayers and Lee Watson.

Karen Young had to move out of the area because hate mail and smear campaigners disrupted her life. Her role was alleged to have been somehow to distract Viv, and this was the reason she was arrested. Police believed they had witnesses strong enough to testify in court that she had some involvement. Karen was kept in custody on two occasions for stringent questioning, but she stood her ground.

Alan Wheat was no longer wanted for questioning. Watson, Sayers and Mr Young were fully questioned and released. Karen Young, Darren Arnold, Alan Jackson and Brian

William Tait were eventually told by the Crown Prosecution Service that there was no case against them.

Those arrested and later released were only suspects and there is no implication that they were involved in the killing. The CPS had to consider the following: the car used in the drive-by shooting had been stolen from Birtley and the area it was stolen from was beside a gym that was allegedly used by a female stripper with whom Darren Arnold was allegedly having a relationship.

A witness had given a description to the police that matched one of those arrested, but, frightened of a reprisal, this witness could not take the stand. Other witnesses were considered to have too significant a criminal record to be able to stand cross-examination.

After Lee Shaun Watson, 32, pleaded guilty to the murder of Freddie Knights, who was murdered in Newcastle on 20 September 2000, he went Queen's Evidence against five other local men.

It is alleged that the payment for the hit on Viv was a bag of cocaine. Viv was no longer around and what the police had to consider was, who would be trying to take over the nightclub doors? This bid for control of the doors never came, and the power vacuum could not be filled, although a feeble attempt was made to do so.

Finally, a selection of views on Viv's murder by some of those closest to him.

Sharon Tate, the sister of Viv's fiancée, Anna Connelly, said, 'With his uncanny knack of being able to spot a pinhead of trouble starting in the darkest of nightclub corners, on the night of his death when a gun was aimed at him, Viv must have been in a world of his own. It was even suggested that he had been spiked in an effort to slow his reactions. I just can't fathom that out, not for the life of me. Viv was told, if he ever went to his car and the tyres were down or the windows were out, to get away from it.'

Anna Connelly said, 'If I could say something to those people who killed Viv, it would be this: why did you want to kill him? Why didn't you shoot him in the legs and make him a cripple? Why use a gun so powerful as that? They tell me just the force of that bullet is enough to kill you. A .357 Magnum didn't need three bullets. Why didn't you just get out and just break his legs, because what did he ever do to deserve this? Out of all the millions of guns, why did the killers choose a Magnum, when a .22 would have got the message across? I knew that, if they shot and they missed, Viv would have been in jail today for murder, because he would have killed them.'

Viv's girlfriend Gillian Lowes said it was frightening to be involved with a man who could be injured or even dead at any time and whom she knew people would always want to have a fight with, but she did not think he would be murdered and maybe one day he would get out of it all. She knew Viv was not invincible, but the way his life suddenly ended shocked her. The problem was that Viv did not have 'fear' in his dictionary; he did not know the meaning of the word.

Gillian hoped that, if the person responsible for his death was married or had a family, their family would never have to go through what hers went through, and said that they may not have known the consequences of what they did. She added that she did not know if they had wanted to kill Viv or simply warn him off.

Peter Connelly recalled, 'After I had heard about it, I just wanted to walk, I was crying, I just wanted to walk and keep walking. Suppose I walked to London and I walked back and someone would tell me that he was all right, that's what I felt like doing. We didn't really think about who did it at the time; it was more or less the next day we said that somebody knew. There had to be a Judas among them.'

19
GETTING AWAY WITH MURDER?

Another unsolved murder, I believe, holds the key to the identity of Viv Graham's killers. Two men murdered 25-year-old Paul Logan, a pizza-delivery driver from Shotley Bridge, two nights before Christmas 1993, seven days before Viv was shot.

Joe Marshall, a convicted gunman, gave evidence to the police, naming the alleged killers of Paul Logan. A further claim is that £5,000 was paid to the two men to beat Paul up, but they went too far and accidentally killed him.

The Geordie Mafia grapevine has it that one of two killers is definitely a heavyweight informant who gets away with selling drugs under the watchful eye of the police, while it is claimed that the second man is said to have served a term in prison for offences of violence. To date, neither man has been charged in connection with Paul Logan's murder.

In a twist to the tale, PC Jeff Hunt, 33, received a three-month prison sentence for misconduct as a public official following an arson attack on a van belonging to Hugh Logan, father of the dead Paul. The man responsible for the petrol-bombing, Keith Suddick, 36, was jailed for carrying out the attack in Shotley Bridge.

To supply information on the murder of Viv Graham or any other murder, contact Crimestoppers, which is run by civilians, on Freephone 0800 555 111. The bigger they are, the harder they fall! High-ranking criminals are seemingly falling over themselves to be as helpful to the police over the Viv murder as they can ... but only in order to receive more lenient prison sentences if caught for serious crimes.

David Glover Jnr gave a statement to the police about Viv's murder, but it was pure invention, designed to help him get away with his dastardly crime of kidnapping and torturing small-time criminal Billy Collier. Glover had high hopes of acting as a supergrass and anticipated that he would walk free from court for his own vicious crime.

At Glover's trial, the then Detective Chief Inspector Felton put in a statement (known as a 'text') to the court on behalf of the accused, confirming that Glover had been working as an informant for Northumbria Police since September 1992 under the pseudonym of Adrian Scott. Glover's job was to gather information about the Conroy family and others.

Later the promoted Superintendent Keith Felton explained that Glover had said things in relation to the Viv murder, but that Glover was not right in the head and could not be believed. After he was imprisoned, Glover still made a bid for further help in having his sentence cut. He was interviewed by two visiting police officers, Detective Constables J Bower and A Trotter, at HM Prison Birmingham on Wednesday 22 February 1995 at 1.30pm:

The interviewing officers reported at the time Glover gave this account that he was in a restraining body belt, previously self-inflicted injuries on his wrists and damaged his cell. We pointed out to Glover that in the circumstances any further conversation held on the subject would be with his legal representative. He stated he would be happy to repeat his account and give further details of the incident in an interview in the presence of his solicitor Mr Harrison. He was informed that we would arrange to interview him at the earliest opportunity convenient with his legal representative. At 2.20pm that day the visit with Glover was concluded.'

The murder on 20 September 2000 of small-time Newcastle drug dealer Freddie Knights, 38, is particularly relevant here as it reveals how low those higher echelons of the crime world will stoop when breaking the biggest taboo that exists within their circle ... becoming a supergrass. Within the underworld this act of betrayal is ranked along with paedophilia. So when someone becomes a supergrass it's an absolute certainty that they have not done so out of the goodness of their heart.

Supergrass and self-confessed underworld killer and drug dealer Lee Shaun Watson, 32, from Gateshead, headed the gangland-style hit on small-time cocaine dealer Knights. Scar-faced Watson had hoped to get away with the hit when he heaped the blame on the unsuspecting John Henry Sayers.

John Henry had been released from prison only a short while after serving 11 years of a 15-year prison sentence for what has been claimed was his masterminding and participation in a daring £350,000 robbery.

After leaving prison he had made a concerted effort to go straight, but his application to set up a taxi business was blocked by Northumbria Police, who objected to his holding the operator's licence needed to run such a business.

John Henry is considered to be one of the most poised and unruffled of underworld figures ever to come out of Newcastle. For him, such a setback was not a defeat but merely a temporary brake on his ambition to go straight. Being clean cut and clean living was part of the man's ethos; he abhorred the use of drugs and did not even drink alcohol.

Northumbria Police still considered John Henry Sayers to be their number-one target and, in a most unremitting way, set about maintaining surveillance and updating intelligence reports on him. Unruffled by this renewed vigour in the way he was targeted, John Henry continued to seek out ways to make an honest living.

When Freddie Knights was cruelly gunned down and killed on his mother's doorstep in a shotgun attack, it was to be the start of a lengthy murder inquiry and trial that was to see Lee Shaun Watson, the self-professed joint second in command of a criminal outfit he called the Firm, turn supergrass.

It was on 13 October 2000, only a few weeks after Knights was murdered, that Watson was a passenger in a car driven by Dale Miller when it went through a red traffic light and a passing police car gave chase. Miller and Watson ran off, and when Watson was cornered by the police he had to be hit with a truncheon to disarm him after he threatened officers with a lock knife. After being found in possession of £25,000 worth of heroin, he was given three years in prison. Some would say it was a pretty light sentence.

While he was in jail Watson was visited regularly by his girlfriend, Vanya Alan, who lived in Highfield, just outside of Rowlands Gill where Viv was from. During one of these visits the police covertly recorded what was said between them via a hidden microphone. This is what prompted Watson to admit to the murder of Knights and invent his outlandish story that John Henry was the boss of the Firm and that three others – Michael Dixon, 34, Eddie Stewart, 39, and Dale Miller, 38 – were runners working under him.

During cross-examination by Jonathan Goldberg QC, Watson was asked if the heroin he had been caught with was payment for the hit on Knights.

'No,' he replied.

Mr Goldberg's questioning continued: 'You asked Dale Miller if he would take the rap for these £25,000 worth of drugs?'

'No.'

'You asked Miller to say it was his heroin?'

'No.'

'Do you know a man named Mickey Conroy?'

'Yes.'

'Has he anything to do with drugs?'

'I think so.'

During further cross-examination by Mr Goldberg, Watson told how he took his girlfriend Vanya Alan with him when he test-fired a shotgun he had bought for £120 and that she had also test-fired it in a field.

Mr Goldberg asked Watson about an incident on 4

September 2000, only 16 days before the killing of Knights, when Watson attacked a property at Hardman Gardens, Ryton, Gateshead.

Mr Duff, for the prosecution, said: 'Kathleen Median, the occupant, had a partner who was a supposed drug dealer. When the house was vacated at 12.15pm, Watson ransacked the house. Firing shots from a 410 sawn-off shotgun into the headboard of the bed [twice] and shooting out a window and a mirror as well as ripping sinks out. Within half an hour, the police called to a house that Watson was in; he was seen to pedal away on a bicycle. Watson evaded capture until 15 September. Further evidence that Watson had been in the property was found in fingerprint evidence.'

Watson admitted to being a career criminal and that his earnings from drug dealing, racketeering and pimping netted him £175,000 per year. He admitted that Knights's little empire would have earned the Firm £100,000 a year when the dealer was ousted from the council estate he supplied.

Mr Goldberg said to Watson, 'I suggest you're a ruthless man and are prepared to shoot someone if you can get away with it?'

'Once Freddie was shot in the leg I would take over the drug dealing on the estate,' Watson testified.

He was asked, 'Mickey Conroy, you knew he dealt in drugs … Did he ever suggest taking over Freddie Knights's estate as far as drug dealing was concerned?' Whereas previously he had said he knew Mickey Conroy, this time he answered, 'I don't know Mickey Conroy.'

Watson was digging himself into a deep hole. On 8 March 2002 he entered a plea of 'guilty' to the charge of murdering

Knights; this was in order to accommodate him as a prosecution witness. Watson's remaining co-defendants had all entered 'not guilty' pleas. So it must have been a daunting prospect for Watson when he considered playing this game of the badly-done-by hitman.

During his session in the witness box, Watson was given break after break after break. In total, he could not have spent more than 12 hours in the dock over a four-day period. When his girlfriend, Vanya Alan, gave evidence, she admitted that the police had given her a sum in the region of £25,000 to assist her and her mother in witness-protection payments.

Heroin addict and gang member Stephen Carlton escaped the wrath of the law when he received a healthy payout of £23,000 from Northumbria Police and escaped robbery charges when he gave evidence against those that he should have been standing next to. Carlton housed some of the gang members after the killing. Yet he walked free!

'Mickey Conroy got Lee Watson to murder Viv Graham after Viv had beaten him up in a fight on Newcastle's Quayside,' said John Henry from the witness box of Leeds Crown Court. A remarkably bold statement that took all aback.

This statement certainly seemed to nullify Watson's so-called assisting the police with the Viv murder. Secretly swearing away every top crook's life could, in reality, have been a ploy by Watson to save his own skin.

John Henry, as I predicted from the day he was arrested, walked from that court in Leeds a free man, acquitted of all three charges of violence against him. It was not only John Henry, though, but also another man acquitted of all charges – Tony Leach. Although Leach faced further unrelated charges at Newcastle Crown Court only weeks later, he was subsequently acquitted of all charges.

Mickey Dixon was found guilty of conspiracy to cause grievous bodily harm to Freddie Knights. He received a nine-year prison sentence. As I sat there looking at him from the press gallery, he was the saddest of sights. He used a mobile phone he had bought from and, eventually, given back to Tony Leach. He also stole a car. I hope he wins his appeal.

Dale Miller, the supposed gunman, was found not guilty of murder, but found guilty of manslaughter … 16 years.

Eddie Stewart admitted his role as getaway driver. Not guilty of murder, but guilty of manslaughter …13 years.

The finale came on 2 October 2002. The Honourable Mr Justice Douglas Brown, a decent sort of judge, vacated Watson's plea of guilty to murder and accepted a plea of guilty to manslaughter. Eleven years in prison, with a life on the supergrass wing, was Watson's lot.

The cost of the inquiry and the trial was said to have been between £15 and £20 million – all taxpayers' money down the drain.

20
AFTER DUFFY

The removal of Duffy cleared the way for further gangland activities. The following piece, from May 2002, appears with thanks to the *Teesside Evening Gazette* and its chief reporter, Angus Hoy: 'A Teesside contract killer who was jailed for life for a double murder is facing a further hefty sentence for his role at the head of a major drugs gang.

'Paul (James) Bryan was found guilty of shooting former Sheffield Eagles Rugby League player David Nelson, 38, and his friend Joseph Montgomery, by a jury at Leeds Crown Court.

'At a court hearing on Teesside earlier this year, Bryan, 41, formerly of Church Lane, Eston, admitted conspiring to supply Class A and B drugs across the North-East.

'Bryan, who was once accused of plotting to murder notorious Teesside hard man Lee Duffy, will be sentenced with six henchmen at Teesside Crown Court in the near future.

'Bryan's gang were tracked by the elite National Crime Squad as they trafficked large quantities of cocaine, heroin, cannabis and amphetamines.

'The two-year Operation Casper inquiry uncovered a lucrative dealing network – with a second-hand-car business as a "front" – stretching as far afield as Northampton and Merseyside.

'During Bryan's murder trial, the court heard how debt-ridden Mr Nelson was gunned down by a masked man in the Wilson's Arms pub in Seacroft, Leeds, on July 22 last year while a children's party was taking place.

'His brother, Andrew Nelson, witnessed the shooting and was also shot at when he ran towards Bryan, but managed to dive to safety.

'As Bryan fled the pub, Mr Montgomery, 40, "courageously" threw a beer glass at him but was fired upon and was also fatally wounded.

'Bryan, whose address was given in court as Bierstow Street, Blackpool, denied murdering Mr Nelson and Mr Montgomery and the attempted murder of Andrew Nelson.

'He was given two life sentences for the murders and ten years for the attempted murder. Bryan smirked as he was led from the dock.

'The judge also said, "You were recruited to shoot a man dead by someone who clearly wanted him dead."

'Detective Superintendent Eddie Hemsley, the senior investigating officer, described Bryan as a very dangerous man who had shown himself to be callous, calculating and a ruthless killer.

'Why Paul Bryan swapped a lucrative drug-dealing empire

for the high-risk world of the contract killer remains a mystery.

'Alongside his life sentence for the Leeds pub murders, he also now faces a lengthy stretch for drug trafficking.

'He was one of seven men convicted at Teesside Crown Court in January this year [2002] of running a nationwide network supplying cocaine, heroin, cannabis and amphetamines.

'To the outside world, Bryan was a second-hand-car dealer, running his business from his home in Church Lane, Eston.

'What he didn't know was that the National Crime Squad – with help from Cleveland Police – had had him under surveillance since June 1998 as part of Operation Casper.

'Bugs were also placed in his car to monitor his frequent trips to Merseyside where he had regular meetings with underworld figures.

'The information gleaned from recorded conversations was damning and left him with no choice but to admit conspiracy to supply.

'His co-defendants included his brother Andrew, also from Eston, who admitted conspiracy to supply Class B drugs.

'Detective Chief Inspector Dave Wright, of the National Crime Squad, said, "Paul Bryan ran his organisation from a safe distance, letting others take the risk of getting arrested as they carried out his orders.

'"This was a particularly lengthy investigation as we were working to gather evidence against a drugs supply network which was highly organised and gave little away.

'"The listening device evidence proved damning against Paul Bryan, as it revealed the true nature of his illegal business – making money from the misery of drugs and not caring about the consequences it wreaked on people's lives."

'One former detective, who had many dealings with Bryan, said he had gradually built up from petty thieving to robberies and drugs.

'In the mid-80s, Bryan and a sidekick were caught targeting post offices, rigging alarms with foam to break in.

'"We locked them up, but he used to say he was mentally ill," said the officer.

'"He would take the blame and was given an indeterminate sentence in a mental hospital.

'"But as soon as he was sentenced, he asked to be examined again and got himself released almost immediately – it was a real con."

'In 1991, Bryan was back in court yet again, this time accused of plotting to murder notorious Teesside hard man Lee Duffy. Duffy was blasted at close range with a shotgun at a blues party in Middlesbrough, but survived after emergency hospital treatment to a leg wound.

'However, murder conspiracy charges against Bryan and six others were dropped in June 1991, at a committal hearing.

'Bryan had hoped to cash in on the affair by suing Cleveland Police for wrongful arrest, but pulled out when a claim by two of his co-accused [Marnon Thomas and Leroy Fischer] was kicked out in 1999.'

For an update on Ray Mallon, taken from an article of 3 May 2002, my thanks go again to Angus Hoy of the *Teesside Evening Gazette*:

'A Teesside man accused of killing a professional rugby player and another man yesterday claimed in court that former Middlesbrough CID chief Ray Mallon threatened to plant a shotgun on him and forced him to sell drugs.

'But under cross-examination, Paul Bryan was accused of making "outlandish, outrageous allegations" to create a "smokescreen".

'Bryan ... said Mr Mallon told him to sell drugs that he had taken from police stores or from people he had arrested.

'He also claimed Mr Mallon had threatened to plant a sawn-off shotgun on him unless he "grassed" on another man.

'Bryan told the jury the charges related to speed and Ecstasy, which had been given to him by Mr Mallon.

'During cross-examination, Jeremy Richardson QC, for the prosecution, said, "You make all sorts of accusations against a person in this trial who can't defend himself, with journalists and all sorts present and just make as many outlandish, outrageous allegations as you can possibly muster. That's your game, isn't it?"

'"No, sir," Bryan replied.'

Referring to Mr Mallon's rebuttal of Bryan's claim, Angus Hoy wrote: 'Middlesbrough Mayor Ray Mallon has spoken out for the first time over "outrageous" claims that he had used double-killer Paul Bryan as a drug dealer.

'The murderer's allegations were also dismissed by the senior detective who led the murder hunt.

'During his defence, Bryan claimed the former head of Middlesbrough CID had forced him into a life of crime.

'The 41-year-old called Mr Mallon "evil" and claimed he had threatened to plant a shotgun on him unless he dealt drugs for him.

'The claims came on the eve of the ballot for Mayor of Middlesbrough in which Mr Mallon was standing.

'Mr Mallon, who won the mayoral battle by a landslide,

said today that Bryan's tactics were a legacy of the Operation Lancet investigation into alleged malpractice in Middlesbrough CID.

"'I have become used to smear and dirty tricks over the past few years, so it came as no surprise to find claims like this coinciding with the election campaign.

"'I'm sure that in the future we will see other criminals jumping on the bandwagon Lancet has set rolling. Fortunately the public of Middlesbrough are not so naive as to be taken in.'"

A friend of Lee Duffy, Lee Harrison, fell prey to the Duffer's curse when he was jailed for nine years in a drugs and prostitution turf war played out in Middlesbrough's seedy town centre sub-culture of drug dealing, drug use and prostitution when he accepted manslaughter charges at Newcastle Crown Court in April 2004.

The involvement of Lee Harrison's father, Tommy, in perverting the course of justice is, it seems, the final twist in this father-and-son story. Tommy was sent to jail for ten years for trying to protect his son, who was mixed up in a drugs and prostitution ring. There are massive complications to this twisting and turning story.

I thank Angus Hoy and the *Teesside Evening Gazette* for being able to unravel the story. The newspaper's coverage starts shortly before 7am on 6 August 2001, at Errol Street, Middlesbrough, where, over 22 hours, one man would die and four would be wounded. 'Chief Superintendent Mark Braithwaite is not the kind of policeman to leave a case unsolved. The scene which confronted him at Errol Street on the morning of August 6 would test his and his team's investigative skills to the limit. Kalvant Singh had fallen to his death, pushed with such force that he plunged through a first-floor bedroom window into the yard below.

'Inside the house, there was a scene of blood-spattered havoc where Michael Moody had been subjected to a savage beating – including having his head smashed into a glass fish tank – that left him needing life-saving surgery.

'The trail then led officers to a seedy bedsit complex less than a mile away in Southfield Road where yet more gratuitous violence had been meted out.

'Gradually, against the twilight backdrop of Middlesbrough's tawdry sub-culture of drugs and prostitution, a picture began to emerge of the people involved and the motives – or lack of them – for their orgy of violence.

'Jonathan Crossling and Thomas Petch had fearsome reputations for violence, while George Coleman, their driver on the night, was a supplier of drugs to, among others, many of the town's working girls.

'Lee Harrison, the son of well-known local businessman Tommy Harrison, was better known as a reggae DJ with no previous history of violence.

'But he was there, both at Errol Street and Southfield Road, and, in the eyes of the investigators, that made him part of the joint enterprise which resulted in Mr Singh's murder.

'Knowing who was there and proving it were two different things, however, and a mammoth and painstaking search began for the evidence needed to bring the guilty men to justice.

'Standing in the way of the investigation were witnesses too afraid to come forward, memories blurred by drug use and the sort of witnesses – prostitutes, criminals drug dealers and the like – hardly guaranteed to convince a jury.

'A further problem arose when it emerged that two of the key suspects – Crossling and Harrison – appeared to have fled the country.

'At the centre of it all was the figure of Kalvant Singh, a 41-year-old market trader ... estranged from his wife; he had been picked up by vice girl Claire Burgess some hours before his death.

'The pair had gone to the Errol Street home of Michael Moody, who regularly let prostitutes use rooms in exchange for cash.

'Burgess had taken drugs, the pair had had a hot drink before going to sleep upstairs, although there was no evidence of sex.

'When Crossling burst through the bedroom door demanding to know where Craig "Dalla" Dalziel was, he is believed to have been high on crack cocaine and simply vented his fury on a stunned Mr Singh.

'Chief Supt Braithwaite remains unable to fathom the few minutes of madness which scarred so many lives for ever: "... Michael Moody was critically injured and still suffers the effects of the attack on him and at least three other people were assaulted.

'"On top of that, a witness is in a long-term relocation programme, two relatively young men are serving life for murder and two others are serving 14 years and nine years for their part in what happened."

'Piece by piece, the team built their case against the accused: specialist forensic experts from London spent more than a week using cutting-edge evidence-gathering techniques at the Errol Street house while vulnerable witnesses were given round-the-clock protection, with one now permanently relocated.

'Months of hard work bore fruit in March 2002, when Coleman and Petch were both jailed for life for murder at Newcastle Crown Court.

'The judge, Mr Justice Turner, said the case was one of the most "sordid and degrading" he had ever dealt with and made a recommendation that Petch serve a minimum of 20 years.

'Crossling, sporting a beard by way of disguise, was tracked down in Benalmadena on Spain's Costa Del Sol with assistance from Interpol and, just before Christmas 2002, Cleveland officers flew out to bring him back ahead of his trial the following June.

'After a dramatic eleventh-hour guilty plea to the lesser charge of manslaughter, he was jailed for a total of 18 years, later reduced to 14 on appeal.

'Lee Harrison, the last of the four, was traced to Jamaica in November last year and Cleveland officers were dispatched in April to bring him back for trial.

'Harrison too opted for a last-minute guilty plea to manslaughter after lengthy discussions with his legal team at Newcastle Crown Court.

'Mr Braithwaite added, "It is without doubt the most challenging, complex and interesting investigation I have led.

'"Every officer involved did a first-class job, they stayed the course from day one and I would like to pay tribute to their skills."'

There the story might end, but Tommy Harrison, the elder

statesman of Teesside's underworld, and the father of Lee Harrison, appeared before Newcastle Crown Court on 10 February 2005, where he was jailed for ten years. Angus Hoy wrote in the *Teesside Evening Gazette* on 11 February 2005:

'The leader of a conspiracy to influence murder trial witnesses and his "principal lieutenant" are behind bars today.

'Tommy Harrison, 62, of Ormesby Bank, Middlesbrough, has been jailed for 10 years and ordered to pay £23,433 legal costs.

'His co-conspirator John "Buster" Atkinson, 55, of Orchard Way, Ormesby, was jailed for four years at Teesside Crown Court yesterday.

'The associates conspired to pervert the course of justice between March 19 and July 1 last year in the then forthcoming trial of Harrison's son Lee, for the killing of market trader Kalvant Singh.

'Judge Peter Fox QC branded Harrison an "inherently devious man", arrogantly disdainful of law officers.

'He told the defendants their conspiracy was the most serious of its type ... They used methods from inducement to threats, property damage, physical violence and coercing one witness to swear a false declaration concocted by Harrison.

'The judge rejected submissions that Harrison, found guilty by a jury, was in poor health and had no assets. He said the source of Harrison's wealth "plainly calls for separate investigation".

'Prosecutor Nicholas Campbell QC said Lee Harrison – identified as part of the gang on the "night of violence" – was later traced to Jamaica.

'Potential witnesses Rowena Frost and Michael Moody,

who was badly injured the night Mr Singh was killed, were approached. Atkinson paid more than £700 for Mr Moody to stay at the Longlands Hotel.

'Documents found at Harrison's home seemed to change Mr Moody's statement to deny the presence of Lee Harrison, who later admitted manslaughter and wounding and was jailed for nine years. Thomas Petch and George Coleman received life sentences for murder, Jonathan Crossling 14 years for manslaughter.'

Keith McQuade's acquittal, in April 2001, of the shotgun slaying of Lee King the previous year led to a 20-month probe into claims that police officers approved a cash loan to an armed robber to buy weapons. As reported in the *Gazette* on 29 July 2005, under the headline 'Lawyers get cash for guns dossier', the following appeared:

'Reports on the long-running Cleveland Police Cash for Guns affair have been passed to the Crown Prosecution Service.

'Keith McQuade was later acquitted of the shotgun murder of Lee King in January 2000 in Park End, Middlesbrough. The CPS will now decide whether any of those involved should face criminal charges.

'Operation Walden was set up to investigate how officers approved the hand-over of £600 to McQuade to buy sawn-off shotguns in December 1999.

'Detectives were told by an informant – named only as "Mr X" – that McQuade was trying to borrow the cash from businessman Joe Livingstone.'

In an article in the *Teesside Evening Gazette* on 7 November 2003, Angus Hoy reported: 'The court had heard how local businessman Joe Livingstone was approached by Keith McQuade in December 1999 who wanted to borrow £600 for weapons.

'The money hand-over was given the go-ahead, but McQuade was not arrested until after the shooting of Lee King in January 2000. He [McQuade] was later cleared of the 32-year-old's [Lee King] murder but is currently serving a life term for armed robbery.

'Police documents revealed that Mr Livingstone had been approached the previous December by Park End armed robber and drug addict Keith McQuade, who wanted to borrow cash to buy sawn-off shotguns.

'The court heard how Mr Livingstone, who runs Pro-line Security from offices in Park End, contacted a Cleveland detective through an intermediary – named in court only as "Mr X" – to ask what he should do. During legal argument, Teesside Crown Court heard that high-level meetings were held involving the then head of Middlesbrough CID Detective Superintendent Adrian Roberts, and the go-ahead was given for Livingstone to hand over the cash.

'But plans to keep McQuade under close armed surveillance went awry …'

'Speaking exclusively to the *Evening Gazette*, Mr Livingstone said, "I want a full public inquiry into the rules and guidelines the police broke and the suppression of evidence.

'"I think Lee King's family also have a right to know what really happened in this case. The police have helped to arm a man they knew to be highly dangerous.

'"I also want to make it absolutely clear once and for all that I am not and never have been a registered police informant."

'James Watson, of Middlesbrough solicitors Watson Woodhouse who represented Mr Livingstone, said, "A detective sergeant has admitted encouraging the unlawful acquisition of a firearm which the police believe may have been used to kill Lee King.

'"If that is true, that officer and the officers who encouraged him are potentially guilty of very serious criminal offences.

'"The Chief Constable ought to urgently examine the case and, if criminal proceedings follow, that will be the appropriate arena in which to examine the rights and wrongs of the matter. If no proceedings follow, the Chief Constable will still have to make clear what role his officers had in the acquisition of firearms and potentially the killing of Lee King.

'"It is also unfortunate that the Chief Constable saw fit to initiate an attempt to try to prevent publication of this material."

'Cleveland Police launched an extraordinary eleventh-hour bid to prevent the *Evening Gazette* revealing the cash for guns scandal.'

I have to praise the *Gazette* for sticking their necks out in this matter, as it was due to their tenacity that this little matter of the police authorisation of cash for guns came to light. I do believe that the family of Lee King could have recourse against the police in this matter, but that is a matter for them to pursue. What is worse than that is how the police allowed such a man as McQuade to purchase a shotgun and then lose track of him!

The *Evening Gazette* further reported: 'Judge Peter Armstrong had "stayed" the trial of 12 men on drugs charges on Wednesday afternoon. But a Contempt of Court Act order

– which prevents the reporting of pre-trial argument until the end of proceedings – remained in place.

'The judge indicated he would lift the order after hearing representation from counsel and the *Evening Gazette*, and prosecutor Steve Williamson QC raised no objection.

'But ... Cleveland Police's head of legal services, Caroline Llewellyn, had called in barrister Nick Wilcox from London to argue that the order should remain in force.

'Mr Wilcox said, "Were you to lift the order at this stage, there is a substantial risk that a particular officer against whom allegations have been made stands a serious risk of being put forward in newspapers in a manner such that he would have no recourse under the law of defamation or of libel."

'Mr Wilcox also told the court other investigations or proceedings were "pending or imminent" and could be damaged by the *Gazette*'s report, but refused to detail them in open court.

'Graham Wood QC, representing Mr Livingstone, dismissed the application: "We are highly suspicious that this may be a contrivance."

'Aidan Marron QC, described the move as a "lamentable situation to have been contrived by the Cleveland Constabulary".

'Paul Cross, for the *Evening Gazette*, told Judge Armstrong: "If the alleged pending proceedings relate to any of the defendants in this case, then the only people likely to be prejudiced by publication are these defendants who are, of course, urging your honour to lift the gagging order."

'After hearing submissions from Mr Wilcox in private, Judge Armstrong ruled: "I am not satisfied that there are pending or imminent proceedings within the meaning of Section 4 (2) of the Contempt of Court Act."

'The court also established that Cleveland Police had no right of appeal to the High Court against the judge's refusal to make an order.'

To date, no police officers have been disciplined over the 'cash for guns' affair. The *Gazette* has to be commended for its unbiased, public interest coverage in this matter.

You may recall that earlier in this book I asked the 'are killers are getting away with murder' in relation to the murder of Julie Hogg, whose body was discovered by her mother, Ann Ming, hidden behind a bath panel at her Billingham home in 1989 – three months after she vanished.

Some 16 years on, Cleveland Police are to reinvestigate the murder.

The double-jeopardy law is outdated; a relic of the Middle Ages. Under measures in the Criminal Justice Act, the law has been amended so that suspects who were acquitted at trial can be brought to court again.

The justice process in any case would still be long-winded, as the Police would have to refer the case to the Chief Prosecutor. The prosecutor would have to then decide if he/she was going to refer the case to the Director of Public Prosecutions. That is when the case could be sent to the Court of Appeal to enable a retrial to be held.

I do stress that a case would only be sent to the Court of Appeal if new and compelling evidence came to light, but who knows how long we will have to wait for that to happen?